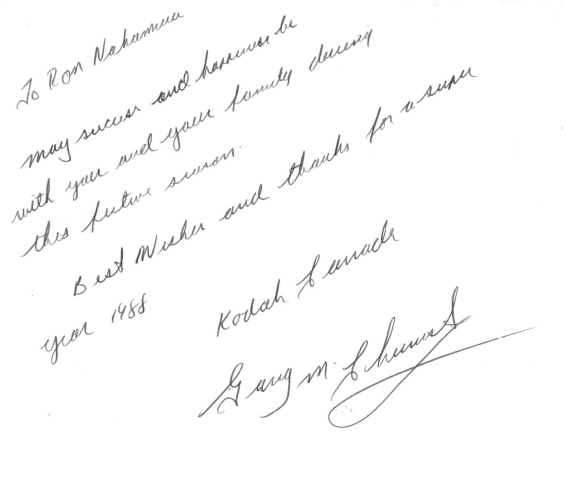

To Ron Nakamura

may success and happiness be
with you and your family during
this future season.

Best Wishes and thanks for a super
year 1988

Kodah Lunach

Gary M. Schwartz

THE OFFICIAL COMMEMORATIVE BOOK

XV OLYMPIC WINTER GAMES

LLOYD ROBERTSON

BRIAN D. JOHNSON

Principal Photographers
OTTMAR BIERWAGEN · IAN TOMLINSON · JIM WILEY

KEY PORTER BOOKS

Canadian Cataloguing in Publication Data

Robertson, Lloyd
    The official commemorative book:
XV Olympic Winter Games

ISBN 1-55013-059-5

1. Winter Olympic Games (15th: 1988: Calgary,
Alta.). I. Johnson, Brian. II. Title.

GV842 1988.R62 1988   796.9'8   C88-093230-9

Acknowledgments

We would like to acknowledge the cooperation
of *Maclean's* magazine in preparing this
book. Special thanks to Kevin Doyle and
Marijke Leupen for access to the *Maclean's*
photographic team.

We would like to acknowledge the support
of Tom Tait and the *Key to Calgary* staff.
Special thanks to CTV, Reuters, and Bob
Carroll/Canada-Wide for their assistance.

Editor: Jennifer Glossop
Photo editor: Susan Renouf
Designer: Marie Bartholomew
Jacket Design: Tony Kennedy GWA Group
Assistant editor: Jennifer MacLeod

Typesetting: Duffoto Process Co. Ltd.
Printing: D.W. Friesen & Sons

Printed and bound in Canada

Official Marks and Symbols
Ⓜ Official Mark
© Canadian Olympic Association 1979

PAGE i:
Canada's Rob Boyd in the Super G.

PAGE ii:
Brian Orser carries the flag in front of the
Canadian team at the Opening Ceremony.

RIGHT:
Colorful balloons rise over McMahon Stadium.

FOLLOWING PAGE:
Karen Percy with her two bronze medals.

Since 1896, the modern Olympics have been the pinnacle of athletic excellence. In February 1988, people around the world focused their attention on Calgary to witness the excitement and color of the many events that were part of the XV Olympic Winter Games.

The Official Commemorative Book: XV Olympic Winter Games provides a permanent record of those days. The pageantry of the Olympic Arts Festival and the opening and closing ceremonies, the personal moments of friendship, and the shared spirit of internationalism are all vividly portrayed through the text and photographs. In these pages, you will find a record of individual and national pride, grace and toil, victory and defeat.

The Calgary Games were the culmination of the efforts of thousands of dedicated staff and volunteers working years before the opening ceremonies, during the Games themselves, and after the Olympics were over. This has truly been a people's Games, for the athletes and for international sport.

I wish to take this opportunity to congratulate the people of Calgary on their dedication, enthusiasm, and the gracious hospitality they exhibited. They have truly demonstrated an Olympian spirit.

Brian Mulroney
Prime Minister of Canada

All the years of planning and hard work by athletes and volunteers, coaches and organizers, corporations and governments, and families and fans; all those years of anticipation; all the hopes and dreams of Olympic glory; all of it came down to two weeks in February 1988 in Calgary, Alberta.

And now that Calgary '88 has become the newest, brightest chapter in Olympic history, it is important that the vivid memories and proud accomplishments of this great cross section of participants be captured for all to relive in the pages of this attractive volume, *The Official Commemorative Book: XV Olympic Winter Games.*

Calgary '88 was a unique celebration of competitive excellence and athletic integrity played out against a canvas of Olympic traditions and Canadian culture. The Government of Canada will long cherish its role as a proud Olympic partner.

Otto Jelinek
Minister of State
Fitness and Amateur Sport

Cathy Priestner and Ken Read carry the Olympic flame to Robyn Perry.

The XV Olympic Winter Games of 1988 will never be forgotten in the Province of Alberta. No other single event has ever generated such enthusiasm, energy, and pride in Albertans, and indeed in Canadians. This commemorative book captures that spirit and enthusiasm.

The new friendships and understanding generated by the experience of hosting the XV Olympic Winter Games can truly be added to the many other Olympic legacies. Personal memories of the years of preparation, the top international competitions which served as test events, the pageantry, the festivities, and of course the people are all preserved with photographs and text and recorded as the Olympic spirit for future generations.

Courage, stamina, and dedication to win honor for their country are dramatized in photographs of the athletes who had earned the right to test their skills at the pinnacle of international competition. Some of these key moments in competition at the XV Olympic Winter Games are reflected in "Olympic Highlights."

The Arts Festival at the XV Olympic Winter Games in Calgary was one of the largest cultural components ever held in conjunction with an Olympic Winter Games. Performers and artists from around the world shared the spotlight at the festival, providing a showcase of creativity and talent.

The Province of Alberta continues to support the keen spirit of competition and expresses its admiration for the physical and creative talent preserved in this official record of the 1988 Olympic Winter Games.

Don R. Getty
Premier of Alberta

The Calgary Tower alight for the Games.

For the world, the XV Olympic Winter Games began February 13 and ended February 28. For Calgarians the dream of staging these Games—the greatest festival of sports and arts—began in the fifties, and the legacy will live for years to come.

The tremendous community support for the Games was a key element in our final successful bid. This support never faltered and grew into an enthusiastic esprit de corps shared by all our citizens. We, as host city, were proud to welcome the world to our festive, banner-clad city and to share with visitors our shining moment in history.

The athletes, many of whom you see pictured in this book, told the Olympic story anew. They strove for an excellence of body and mind and tested the limits of their endurance and capabilities. To win an Olympic event is an athlete's finest hour. Many who saw the champions on television later came to the Olympic Plaza to share the excitement and the glory and to witness the nightly medal presentations. On such occasions everyone could participate in the celebration. Although there were many thousands of volunteers working with the city, with OCO'88, and with the sponsors, there were many more Calgarians who simply wanted to share in the spirit of the Games. In this manner even pin-trading became an important sport that anyone could play.

The Olympic Plaza, built with the Olympics in mind, has created a whole new focus for downtown Calgary. Situated opposite City Hall, with a lagoon and fountains in summer and an ice rink in winter, it has brought new vitality to the heart of the city. The Olympic Saddledome, with its award-winning design, was created for the Olympics but, like the plaza, quickly became an essential part of our modern city. Other facilities, like Canada Olympic Park and the Olympic Oval, will become important to the life of Calgary. They are our legacy of the Games. The dream is still alive. These world-class sports venues will provide the finest facilities for training an athlete can have. They will inspire our youth to excel and to become future Olympians. Other related facilities have enriched our lives and, because of the Olympics, were put in place years ahead of schedule.

We are a forward-moving, young, and dynamic city, and we take advantage of our geographical position and pride in our modern facilities. We have a tradition in the west for being optimistic and independent, and we welcome others to our land. We are proud of our place in history as host city of the XV Olympic Winter Games, and we are proud to share these moments with you in this book.

Ralph Klein
Mayor
City of Calgary

Marie Andree Masson of Canada in the 10-kilometre cross-country race.

It has been truly amazing to watch the spirit of the Olympics engulf Canmore, our small mountain community of 4300 people, set in the splendor of the Canadian Rockies. The enthusiasm and commitment of the town's people to the XV Olympic Winter Games has provided the opportunity for growth and vision to become our goal for the future.

The Canmore Nordic Centre was officially opened in December 1986. The centre was immediately the focus of international attention, hosting three World Cups in the first three months of operation. Athletes, coaches, and spectators flooded Canmore with praise for the centre and town facilities. Canmore Nordic Centre has proven to be a huge success with recreational and high-performance athletes alike. The Olympic events that took place here are a perfect start for Canmore's future as the nation's host to major Nordic events.

Canmore Olympic Village was developed to house more than 600 athletes, coaches, and officials. Almost entirely self-sufficient, the village provided accommodation and on-site retail and recreational outlets. Its first-class recreational facilities, which include a swimming pool, curling rink, and golf clubhouse, are a legacy that will be enjoyed by residents and visitors alike.

Less than a decade after the Canmore coal mines were closed down, we are looking forward to achieving our tourism and recreational goals, goals that have been greatly expedited by the Olympic focus and legacy.

Most important, the Olympics instilled a spirit of cooperation and friendship in the town of Canmore. Hundreds of volunteers committed themselves to making the Olympics a positive and rewarding experience for participants and spectators. The people of Canmore will remember forever their exciting role in the 1988 Olympic Winter Games, and they welcome the world to the Rocky Mountains.

Paula Andrews
Mayor
Town of Canmore

CONTENTS

THE OLYMPIC SPIRIT

FRANK KING, CHAIRMAN, XV OLYMPIC WINTER GAMES ORGANIZING COMMITTEE

Special memories, special moments, and special friends. We shared them all during the XV Olympic Winter Games. The emotion of the Olympic torch relay, the grace and energy of the Olympic Arts Festival, and the triumph and disappointment of Olympic competition—each touched us with its power, each filled us with the Olympic spirit.

Whether you were a Team '88 member, a spectator, or a proud Canadian watching the Games at home, this book was written to help you recapture the incredible feeling that swept through the City of Calgary and across our country for sixteen wonderful days in February 1988.

I was privileged to serve as chairman of the XV Olympic Winter Games Organizing Committee—a dedicated group of nearly 10 000 volunteers and staff known as Team '88. Each day presented an exciting new challenge as Team '88 worked toward our goal of hosting a Winter Games that would be recorded in Olympic history as the finest ever staged.

Although a decade has passed since a small group of people began working to help bring the 1988 Olympic Winter Games to Calgary, it was on the afternoon of September 30, 1981, that the city's Olympic dream became a reality. On that day at Baden-Baden, Federal Republic of Germany, International Olympic Committee president Juan Antonio Samaranch proclaimed Calgary host city of the XV Olympic Winter Games. It was a moment none of us will forget.

Looking back, it's difficult to believe Calgary had little in the way of Olympic-calibre winter sports facilities when it was awarded the Games. But what we lacked in facilities we more than made up for in talented people—people with the collective determination to host the best-ever Games.

Today, Calgary is recognized as a world leader in the sports of ice and snow. It's been a dizzying transformation for this young, vibrant city of 640 000. Indeed, the 1988 Winter Games have left Calgary a legacy of world-class winter sports facilities, funded by OCO'88 and its three government partners.

One of the earliest challenges faced by the organizing committee was funding. More money was spent on the 1988 Winter Olympics than any other winter sporting event in Canadian history. But with the generous financial support of the Government of Canada, the Province of Alberta, and the City of Calgary—combined with financial contributions from the television rights' holders and nearly a hundred official sponsors, suppliers, and licensees—the XV Olympic Winter Games will long be remembered as an event that did not burden local taxpayers.

Young Robyn Perry stands beside the rising Olympic cauldron.

OCO'88's financial partners should be proud of their participation and role in the Winter Olympics. The successful combination of government and private enterprise financing is undoubtedly one of the great success stories of the 1988 Winter Games.

In addition, the Games helped provide a legacy of endowment funds for the benefit of Canadian amateur sport. Through its financial support of amateur athletics, millions of dollars in endowments will aid in the development of future Canadian Olympians for years to come. In this way, the spirit of the XV Olympic Winter Games will remain in the hearts of future generations. The Games also helped provide the Calgary and Canmore regions with many direct economic benefits. Increased levels of tourism will revitalize the local economies, promoting investment which will provide employment opportunities that otherwise would not have existed.

The XV Olympic Winter Games will also be remembered for many firsts. Calgary was the first Canadian city to host the Winter Olympics, and with sixteen full competition days, the 1988 Games were also the longest-running in history. Other firsts included the use of a fully enclosed 400-metre speed skating oval and the largest ice hockey crowds in Olympic history.

Of course, the record number of participants the Games attracted was another great success story, as were the record numbers of athletes, volunteers, and spectators who all played important roles in making the 1988 Olympic Winter Games such an overwhelming success.

For the more than 9000 volunteers and nearly 500 staff members of Team '88, the XV Olympic Winter Games also provided a once-in-a-lifetime opportunity to help shape an important part of Canadian sporting history. The Games were richer for the thousands of people who helped celebrate the Olympic spirit by participating in the torch relay, attending an Arts Festival event, or watching the sports competitions.

But Calgary's Olympic celebration would not have been possible were it not for the singular vision of an idealistic French aristocrat. It was Pierre de Coubertin who brought us the modern Olympic Games. De Coubertin saw the ancient Greeks' love of competition and belief in the development of physical health and skill as qualities well worth preserving in the modern world. His vision, which today is celebrated by people around the world, is clearly reflected in the ideals of the Olympic movement.

The fundamental aims of the Olympic movement are simple. They are to promote the development of those physical and moral qualities that are the basis of sport; to educate young people through sport in a spirit of friendship and of better understanding between each other; to spread the Olympic principles throughout the world, thereby creating international goodwill, and to bring together the athletes of the world every four years in the great sports festival, the Olympic Games.

The athletes who participated in the 1988 Olympic Winter Games lived up to these ideals through their achievements and conduct on the field of competition. Although not all won Olympic gold, all athletes performed to the best of their abilities. In doing so, they exhibited the highest expression of the true Olympic spirit. This same drive–to be the best you can be–was shared by many other people who helped host the best-ever Games. The members of Team '88, the residents of Calgary, the people of Alberta, and every Canadian who supported the Olympic dream–together we endeavored to live up to the ideals of the Olympic movement.

From the beginning, there was always a strong desire at the organizing committee to pass on the Olympic ideals to a special group of people–Alberta's schoolchildren. To achieve this goal, OCO'88 instituted a unique Youth and Education program which developed a series of informative Olympic resource kits. Later, with the help of the Government of Canada and the Canadian Olympic Association, these highly successful resource kits were distributed to schoolchildren nationwide, helping to strengthen Canada's Olympic future in both the Olympic spirit and the legacy of the 1988 Olympic Winter Games.

In many ways we have all helped further the Olympic ideals. Together we worked to attain excellence by promoting greater peace, friendship, and international goodwill through sport for sixteen days in February 1988. Ultimately, this will stand as the greatest legacy of the XV Olympic Winter Games. Both Calgary and Canada will long be remembered for the hand held out to their friends around the world. We have helped make this world a better place to live, and through the friendship of people, we helped spread the Olympic spirit.

The flags of competing nations.

OLYMPIC HIGHLIGHTS

PRECEDING PAGES:
Swiss skiing star Maria Walliser.

TOP LEFT:
Team USA against the Soviets.

LEFT:
The Soviet hockey team wins gold.

TOP:
In the spotlight: Debi Thomas of the USA.

ABOVE:
Brian Boitano shows off his gold medal.

RIGHT:
Brian Orser in the long program.

FAR LEFT:
Vreni Schneider in her gold medal slalom run.

TOP:
Matti Nykanen, the Flying Finn, only male athlete to win three golds.

LEFT:
The superb Canmore biathlon course.

ABOVE:
A gold medal was waiting for Hubert Strolz in alpine combined.

LEFT:
Tracy Wilson and Rob McCall, a bronze for Canada.

TOP:
Alberto Tomba, winner of the giant slalom.

ABOVE:
Reigning champion Katarina Witt.

RIGHT:
A surprise contender—Midori Ito of Japan.

PRECEDING PAGES:
Canada was out of the running for a gold with its loss to the USSR.

LEFT:
The crowd-pleasing Jamaican bobsleigh team.

TOP:
Ekaterina Gordeeva and Serguei Grinkov win a gold.

ABOVE:
Gold medalist Bonnie Blair of the USA.

RIGHT:
Tomas Gustafson set new records in speed skating.

LEFT:
Elisabeth Gerg of the Federal Republic of Germany.

TOP LEFT:
Leendert Visser of the Netherlands.

TOP RIGHT:
Yvonne van Gennip, winner of three gold medals.

ABOVE:
Gaetan Boucher in his last Olympic speed skating competition.

ABOVE:
Tamara Tikhonova and her teammates are congratulated by the Finnish team after the 4-x-5-kilometre cross-country relay.

LEFT:
Victory on the slopes: Peter Mueller, Pirmin Zurbriggen, and Franck Piccard.

RIGHT ABOVE:
Bronze medalist Karen Percy in a pensive moment.

RIGHT:
A silver finish for Elizabeth Manley.

DAY 1

After a decade of preparation, the time finally arrived. On a cold, windy afternoon under a generous patch of blue sky, 60 000 people had gathered to bear witness to the Olympic spirit. And through the magnifying glass of television's global village, a football stadium in the foothills of the Rocky Mountains could reach another two billion viewers. In an extravagant spectacle, wave upon wave of pageantry dazzled the eye — battalions of dancers created living kaleidoscopes; flocks of balloons and pigeons swirled into the north wind; and athletes paraded past in costumes that ranged in color from Sweden's cool blue to Bolivia's Day-Glo green. It was a day on which Alberta's western culture occupied the centre of the world stage. Cowboys twirled lassos. Feather-headdressed chiefs charged into the stadium at full gallop. Harnessed thoroughbreds dragged chuckwagons that skidded around barrels. The focus was also on Canada, as Mounties on black horses pranced with royal precision in honor of Governor-General Jeanne Sauvé. But the Governor-General's declaration that the XV Olympic Winter Games were officially open did not relieve the suspense. For Canadians the anticipation of the Games was to culminate in a single event: the arrival of the Olympic torch. The torch was the Olympic spirit made tangible. Blazing a trail from ancient Greece to the New World — from Prometheus to Petro-Canada — it galvanized the country. Two of Canada's Olympic veterans, Barbara Ann Scott and Ferd Hayward, had begun the torch relay in a blizzard in St. John's, Newfoundland, on November 17. Three months and 18 000 kilometres later, the flame was handed to "a future Olympian," a twelve-year-old figure skater from Calgary named Robyn Perry. To the rising beat of native drums, she bounded up the steps to the altar. She stretched to reach the edge of the cauldron. Then, as the crowd roared, she ignited a flame that was beyond anyone's grasp, yet large enough for all the world to share.

The Olympic flag, its five rings symbolizing the five major areas of the world, was raised to the refrain of the Olympic anthem. As the flag reached the top of the mast, one thousand pigeons were released at the south end of the stadium.

Opening Ceremony

An outline of the dove of peace capped the performance by a group of youngsters in shimmering blue. Everyone in the audience had been issued a poncho, which turned each spectator into a color-keyed pixel in a human canvas of Olympic heraldry.

"The dream has become a reality." With those words, OCO'88 chairman Frank King evenly summed up Day One's sense of accomplishment. The celebration began at one o'clock in McMahon Stadium, which had undergone a face-lift and an expansion with scaffolds of bleachers that added an extra 20 000 seats. A two-day chinook had warmed Calgary to above-freezing temperatures, but winter returned promptly for the opening ceremony. Flags snapped in a chill wind that whistled right through the makeshift bleachers.

At the core of the pageant was the athletes' parade. Each team offered its own fashion statement, flashes of eccentricity tempering the official symmetry of the event. The Argentinians wore woolen ponchos. The Italians, the French, and the Americans found a common trend in stylish trenchcoats and fedoras. The Federal Republic of Germany paraded as a pastel vision in lilac and green. The Soviet Union was wrapped in fur. And a big cheer went up for the Jamaican bobsledders, who seemed to saunter rather than march around the stadium in their canary-yellow parkas. The Canadian team was the last to appear, wearing white Stetsons, scarlet coats, and fringed shoulder pads decked with maple leaves. It was a case of unadulterated Canadian identity. Electricity shot through the crowd as a jubilant Brian Orser carried the flag into the arena. Eventually, when all the athletes had filed into seats

The druidic robed members of the Olympic Ceremonies Choir created an almost ominous presence as their vivid colors separated into the Olympic rings.

BELOW RIGHT:
Members of the aboriginal people of Alberta—the Sarcee, Blackfoot, Blood, Peigan, and Stoney tribes—thundered into the stadium on horseback as part of a program celebrating the province's cultural diversity.

above the dais, their ranks formed ribbons of color in a rich but random flag of their own making.

There were moments when emotion transcended spectacle. One was when Ian Tyson and Gordon Lightfoot, strumming guitars, sang "Four Strong Winds" and "Alberta Bound" while dancers whirled through a western two-step. Another was the surprise of hearing "O Canada" sung by an aboriginal Canadian singer in the blunt-edged syllables of Tutoni, a language unfamiliar to most of the audience. But one of the most memorable moments was when a thousand children swarmed into the stadium. Wearing costumes of a remarkable iridescent blue, they mimed images of Olympic sports. For cross-country skiing they danced a lively shuffle; for luge they formed a snaking chain, then collapsed on their backs like dominoes. The choreography was clever, but what was most striking about the children was their sheer exuberance. Jumping and jiving through their routines, they offered the ideal antidote to the pomp and circumstance of the occasion. And, of course, it was a child who had the honor of delivering the Olympic flame to its final destination. Young Robyn Perry received the torch from two Calgarians, former World Cup ski champion Ken Read and silver-medal speed skater Cathy Priestner. As she mounted the steps to the cauldron, she seemed carried up on the energy of the crowd.

That night the flame spread to downtown Calgary. Traffic jammed the streets; fireworks and lasers lit the sky, and people craned their necks to see a fire burning atop the Calgary Tower, transforming it into a huge torch. The celebration had hit the streets. The Games were on. Now it was up to the athletes to bring the Olympic spirit back to earth.

Hundreds of dancers in western garb filled McMahon Stadium with a swirl of color and soon had the audience clapping along with their sprightly two-step.

Extending her reach, twelve-year-old Robyn Perry, a "future Olympian," lights the Olympic flame. Eighty-eight torchbearers, one from each day of the 18 000-kilometre cross-Canada relay, participated in this crowning moment.

Hockey

Opening-night hockey saw a shooting match at the Olympic Saddledome, with the United States, in white, beating Austria, in red, 10-6.

The opening day of Olympic competition offered both the predictable and the unexpected. On the predictable side of the ledger was the United States hockey team's 10-6 win over an inexperienced Austrian squad and the Soviet Union's 5-0 drubbing of an underdeveloped Norwegian team—although both victors played well below par. The unexpected result was the Federal Republic of Germany's 2-1 upset over Czechoslovakia. The victory muddied the complexion of the medal round among the six B-pool teams. And it made the Czechs wonder if the West German team had become their eternal nemesis. The upset recalled the puzzling encounter two months earlier between the two teams at the 1987 Izvestia tournament. "We have had problems with the West Germans," moaned Czech coach Jan Starsi after the game in Calgary. "According to the books this shouldn't happen. The players' qualities are better on our side." But in the heat of Olympic competition, the books are obviously not to be trusted.

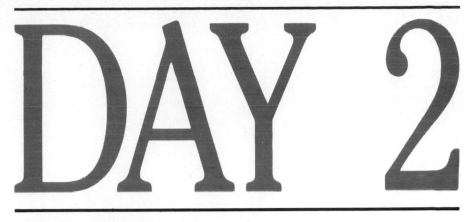

DAY 2

SUNDAY, FEBRUARY 14

It was the first full day of Olympic events — and the athletes' first opportunity to test Calgary's remarkable new ice facilities in Olympic competition. World track records fell at both the luge run and the speed skating oval. But Alberta's changeable weather disrupted the action at Nakiska. Winds of up to 160 kilometres per hour blasted across the face of Mount Allan, forcing postponement of the eagerly awaited men's downhill event. The spotlight shifted instead to the 70-metre ski jump at Canada Olympic Park, where a crowd of 52 000 packed the bowl at the bottom of the run. There, a marvel known as the Flying Finn became the talk of the day. Turning a strong but manageable wind to his advantage, the unrivaled Matti Nykanen soared to gold with the grace of a hawk gliding a mountain updraft. Commentators searched for words to describe his performance — how he found the perfect point of takeoff, how he planed so much farther over his skis than the other jumpers, how he angled boldly into the wind, and how he waited until the last possible moment before making his concession to gravity. But amid all the accolades and explanations, no one really knew how he did it. It was magic. And, as with all good magic, the technique was so serene as to be invisible. Then, in case anyone considered his feat an isolated fluke of circumstance, he did it again. Each time he flew exactly the same distance — 89.5 metres — as if that was exactly how far it was possible to fly that particular day. His closest competitor, Czech jumper Pavel Ploc, landed a full 2.5 metres behind him. Nykanen himself was at a loss to explain his prowess. "I was slightly surprised to be that far ahead of everyone," said the Flying Finn, who has learned never to look back.

Matti Nykanen of Finland watches for the start signal before his remarkable flight in the men's 70-metre ski jump.

Ski Jumping

The Flying Finn soared beyond all competitors in the 70-metre event at Canada Olympic Park. With his matched pair of 89.5-metre jumps, Matti Nykanen eclipsed a noteworthy feat by the Czechs, who won both silver and bronze in the event.

After Nykanen, it was good-humored Eddy "The Eagle" Edwards who stole the show. With his spirited last-place finish, Edwards sailed to one of the most glorious defeats in Winter Olympic history and breathed fresh life into a creed often lost in the scramble for Olympic gold: "The most important thing in the Olympic Games is not to win but to take part." Great Britain's first Olympic competitor in the event, Edwards captured the imagination of millions with his sunny acceptance of mediocrity. To the crowd's rapturous applause, he glided 55 metres to a fifty-eighth-place finish, then raised his skis in triumph. He had, after all, set a British record. Edwards' parents flew in from Britain to watch the event. "I thought about waving to them while I was on the jump," said Edwards, "but I was too busy trying to stand up."

Hockey

Randy Gregg and Zarley Zalapski of Canada flank Marek Stebnick of Poland. Canada clung to its one-point lead throughout this hockey game, its first of the Winter Olympics.

For Team Canada, it was an unnerving way to start an Olympic tournament. After training together for three years, they barely squeaked by a Polish squad that had played together for only five weeks. After the Canadians, grateful for small mercies, concluded their shaky Olympic debut at the Saddledome with their 1-0 victory, Switzerland and Finland took to the ice with surprising results. The dark-horse Swiss team beat the Finns 2-1.

Figure Skating

Petite Ekaterina Gordeeva and Serguei Grinkov of the Soviet Union easily won the pairs short program with their exquisite routine.

The stars lived up to their billing. To the bracing rhythms of *Carmen*, the Soviet Union's royal couple of figure skating, Ekaterina Gordeeva and Serguei Grinkov, spun their way to the highest score of the pairs short program. Sixteen-year-old Gordeeva, a ponytailed sprite reminiscent of Nadia Comaneci, the gamine gymnast who charmed the world during the 1976 Olympics, skated in exquisite unison with her twenty-one-year-old partner. Wearing white outfits shimmering with silver braids and sequins, they moved briskly through a program that began with an ethereal split triple twist and ended with a combination stem in which Gordeeva twirled around Grinkov's waist like a supple vine.

Canadian skaters Denise Benning (in gold lamé) and Lyndon Johnston (in a modified tux) electrified the audience with an energetic routine set to big-band music. "Very entertaining," remarked an American television commentator. "But then, the judges are not there to be entertained." Indeed, the judges didn't seem as thrilled as the audience, although the pair still placed fifth. After the event, Canadian coach Kerry Leitch was furious that one Soviet couple, Larissa Selezneva and Oleg Makarov, managed to finish sixth despite a fall and a slipup. Perhaps the most theatrical of Olympic sports, figure skating also suffers from some of the most violent disagreements over judging. And this day's dispute would, no doubt, not be the last.

Cross-Country Skiing

Strength. Endurance. Determination. Few trials of an athlete's conditioning are as exacting as a cross-country race. And in the 10-kilometre event at Canmore, the Soviet women emerged as the hardest-working athletes on the Olympic stage as they captured four of the top five spots, with Vida Ventsene and Raisa Smetanina taking the gold and silver.

The Canadians had a dismal day. Angela Schmidt Foster, a skier from Midland, Ontario, who was touted as a top-ten contender, rejected the wax chosen by her support crew. Instead, she applied her own combination to her skis before the race. It was the wrong wax for the snow, forcing her to work harder than necessary. She finished thirty-eighth, almost four minutes behind the leader. It was not the first time that the politics of equipment maintenance had negated months of Olympic training. But another race lay ahead. And the show must go on.

Angela Schmidt Foster of Canada is consoled after her thirty-eighth-place finish in the women's 10-kilometre cross-country race.

ABOVE:
The Norwegian fans had something to cheer about: four members of their team placed in the top twenty in cross-country, although none won a medal.

RIGHT:
Her exhaustion showing on her face, Raisa Smetanina of the USSR strides to a second-place finish. Her teammate Vida Ventsene took the gold, a surprise in a sport traditionally dominated by Scandinavian countries.

Speed Skating

Jens-Uwe Mey streaks to a victory in the 500-metre speed skating event. Traveling at an average speed of 49.3 kilometres per hour, Mey became the world's fastest human with his win in the new Olympic Oval.

His arms swinging high at a clockwork tempo, a blue-suited Jens-Uwe Mey skated his way to gold and set a new world record in the 500-metre speed skating event. The East German's feat confirmed claims that Calgary's new speed skating oval—a unique indoor facility—offered skaters a faster track than any in the world.

But a darker drama overshadowed Mey's triumph. Just hours before the race, world sprint speed skating champion Dan Jansen learned that his twenty-seven-year-old sister, Jane, had died in Wisconsin of leukemia. Jansen decided to go ahead with the race, and the U.S. team announced that it would dedicate its performance to his sister. However, as Jansen rounded the first bend of the Oval, he fell, sliding across the ice and upending Japanese skater Yasushi Kuroiwa. Neither man was injured. "It felt like my skate slipped out from under me," said Jansen afterward, "and the next thing I knew I was in the stands." The skater, who talked to his sister by phone just hours before her death, said he intended to pick up the pieces of his Olympic dream on Thursday. "It's very important to my family that I don't go home now—Jane wouldn't have wanted it that way."

Meanwhile, Canada's sentimental favorite, 1984 gold medalist Gaetan Boucher, had a disappointing race. But Quebec City's Guy Thibault emerged as a rising star, placing seventh and breaking the Canadian record with a time of 36.96. For many observers, the ultimate star of the event was the Oval itself, a temperature-controlled rink the size of two football fields. With such a facility as a permanent legacy of the Games, Canada's speed skating power can only be expected to improve.

Guy Thibault prepares for his start in the 500-metre speed skating race. His time of 36.96 broke the Canadian record and put him in seventh place, just over half a second behind Mey.

Luge

Luge is one of the most dangerous winter sports, and to the uninformed spectator the participant appears frighteningly passive to his own fate. But the sport requires intense concentration and great muscular strength. Swathed in their skintight rubberized suits, the lugers are flattened against their sleds by forces that can reach up to seven times the force of gravity. Luge—the name is French for *sled*—is still a novelty in North America. And the masters of the art are European. However, the new luge and bob-sleigh run at Canada Olympic Park could help popularize the sport in Canada. About 22 000 spectators arrived for the unveiling of the run and crowded along the 1200-metre length of the refrigerated concrete track, which snakes down a hillside at the site.

Leading thirty-eight sliders in the first day of men's singles competition was Jens Mueller of the German Democratic Republic. He blazed down the track at an average speed of 117.8 kilometres per hour, breaking his own record on the track, the limits of which have yet to be tested.

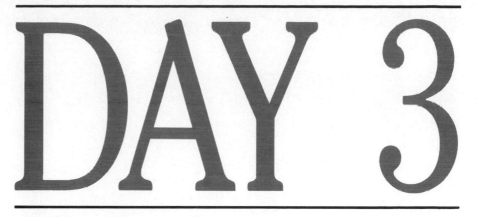

DAY 3

MONDAY, FEBRUARY 15

Men's downhill, the macho event of the Winter Games, consists of a mad descent down a mountain at speeds of up to 120 kilometres per hour. It's all over in two minutes, give or take a few seconds. Once the snow settled following a morning of blistering runs down Mount Allan, only half a second separated gold and silver. Although fifty-one skiers braved the course, it was obvious from the beginning that the event would not be a contest of nations but a duel of individuals — a classic showdown between Swiss superstars Pirmin Zurbriggen and Peter Mueller. Zurbriggen's victory, his first Olympic triumph, gave impetus to his unlikely quest to sweep all five alpine events — breaking the triple-gold record set by France's Jean-Claude Killy in 1968. Ironically, with Franck Piccard taking the bronze at Mount Allan, France finally won its first Olympic medal in the men's downhill since Killy's triumph in Grenoble. But while the Swiss and the French reveled, the Canadians despaired. Rob Boyd of Whistler, British Columbia, who turned twenty-two the day of the race, had little to celebrate; he placed sixteenth. Canada's other hope, Brian Stemmle, skiing while recovering from torn ligaments in his knee, missed a gate and was disqualified. Canada also fared poorly in other events, except for the men's 30-kilometre cross-country, where Quebec's Pierre Harvey placed fourteenth, the best cross-country showing ever by a Canadian skier in the Olympic Games. By now, however, both Canadians and Americans were getting impatient for some Olympic glory. With the Swiss outclassing all comers at Mount Allan, the Soviets almost sweeping cross-country, the East and West German athletes taking the gold and silver in men's luge, and the United States surrendering an important hockey game to Czechoslovakia, there was indeed cause for concern on the third day of the Games: things did not look promising for North America.

Pirmin Zurbriggen, the shy Swiss, flies on his way to beating countryman Peter Mueller by half a second in the men's downhill event.

Alpine Skiing

ABOVE:

Peter Mueller's disappointment at losing the event he hoped most to win shows clearly on his face as he watches teammate Pirmin Zurbriggen's time flash on the scoreboard.

RIGHT:

Pirmin Zurbriggen is jubilant after his stunning gold-medal run in the men's downhill competition.

The two Swiss rivals were a study in contrasts. There was Peter Mueller: rugged, heavy-muscled, aggressive. A star who enjoys the glamour that surrounds him in Europe, he drives a cherry-red Porsche and wears leather pants. Then there was Pirmin Zurbriggen: slender, graceful, shy. A golden-haired country boy from an alpine village, he drives a Mercedes, is a devout Roman Catholic, and is nervous with the press. Above all else, Mueller wanted to win the men's downhill, the prestige event of alpine racing.

After the weather had forced a one-day delay, tensions were running high at Mount Allan. Mueller was the first skier down the course, an unenviable position. But after he completed an apparently flawless run, it was hard to imagine that anyone could do better— until Zurbriggen. The challenger was worried, especially on the steep upper section of the run, where his hand hit the snow twice. Even so, on that section Zurbriggen matched Mueller's time within an amazing one-five-hundredth of a second. On the lower stretch, where skiing is reduced to the aerodynamic art of pure flight, Zurbriggen gained speed. Mueller had said he would be satisfied with nothing less than gold. As his rival's time flashed on the scoreboard, he looked grim. When Zurbriggen saw his time, he cupped his hands for a moment of prayer—then, with his priorities in perfect order, phoned his parents in Switzerland.

Huge crowds flock to the dramatic first race of the alpine events at Nakiska, outside Calgary.

Identified by name, symbol, color, and number, Olympic competitors are easily recognized by television audiences.

Curling

Although it was only a demonstration sport, with no impact on the international medal race, curling provided some solace on a day when Canadian athletes had little else to be proud of. Canada's Ed Lukowich, winner of the 1986 world championship, broke open a teeter-totter game and defeated U.S. curler Bud Somerville 9-5 to a storm of applause. And Canada's Linda Moore fought off a feisty challenge to defeat Switzerland's Cristina Lestander. Moore appeared to be headed for a showdown with her friend Elisabeth Hogstrom of Sweden. Both undefeated with 3-0 records, Moore and Hogstrom met at a bonspiel four years ago.

Cross-Country Skiing

With mild temperatures and lightly falling snow, the conditions on Canmore's grueling 10-kilometre track were tricky. But that didn't stop the Soviet men from striding ahead of the Scandinavian favorites to win silver and gold—neatly bookending their victories at the women's event the previous day. The Soviet team seemed to have found the right wax to grip the course's steep hills, while such stars as Sweden's Gunde Svan and Torgny Mogren complained that their skis were slipping. However, Canada's Pierre Harvey seemed relaxed and confident as he kicked and glided into the Canadian cross-country record book with a fourteenth-place finish. On a day that a sad performance by the country's downhillers was attributed largely to Olympic stage fright, Harvey was unusually calm. "I'm skiing for myself," he explained. "I can't ski for twenty million people."

Hockey

Corey Millen and Allen Bourbeau of the U.S. team share a short-lived triumph in their game against Czechoslovakia, which ended in a 7-5 win for the Czechs.

It was a key game for both the United States and Czechoslovakia. And after staking down an early 3-0 lead, the Americans looked invincible. But, led by team captain Dusan Pasek, the Czechs battled back, overtaking their opponents late in the third period when Pasek scored a goal while killing a penalty. A shot into an empty net made the final score 7-5 for Czechoslovakia.

The Federal Republic of Germany followed their victory against the Czechs with a 7-3 win over Norway in an ill-tempered game that included twenty-two penalties. And the USSR thrashed Austria in an 8-1 game, during which the Soviets scored three goals in just 61 seconds.

RIGHT:
Czech goalie Dominik Hasek lunges for the puck.
After letting in three goals during the first six
minutes of play, Hasek was replaced by Jaromir
Sindel.

BELOW:
The U.S. goalie, Michael Richter, took the loss
against Czechoslovakia hard. The Czechs have
long been a jinx for the American team. Five
times the USA has failed to win an Olympic gold
—and each time they have lost to the Czechs.

FAR RIGHT:
Players try to locate the puck beneath the skates
of Arne Billkvam of Norway. His team lost 7-3 to
the unbeaten Federal Republic of Germany.

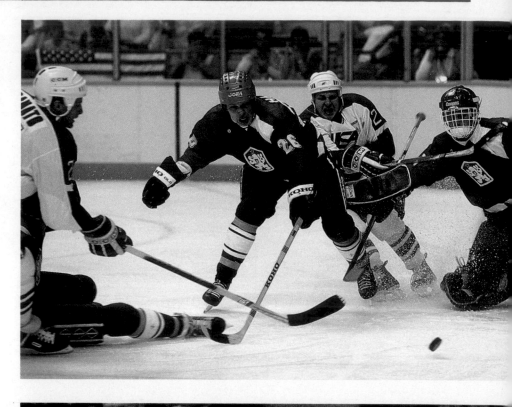

Luge

Paul Hildgartner of Italy starts down the innovative new luge track at Canada Olympic Park to a tenth-place finish. A refrigeration system keeps the track at a constant temperature, but nothing can control the unpredictable winds at the site.

Iouri Khartchenko of the USSR took the bronze medal for luge behind the German Democratic Republic and the Federal Republic of Germany on a day when emotions and winds ran high.

Under the pressure of Olympic competition, athletes sometimes become convinced that their performance can be affected by elements beyond their control. One is the weather. Another is the psychological climate of the athlete. The night before he coasted to gold in the men's singles luge, East German Jens Mueller had trouble sleeping. In the morning, he walked up and down the track, mulling things over. "I didn't feel in control," he said, "until I stepped in the sled." Then the twenty-two-year-old physical education student conquered his nerves—and the competition. West German Georg Hackl, who claimed the silver, complained that a gusting wind got in his way during his third run. Since the winds were relatively calm during Mueller's run, Hackl's coaches launched an official protest that such an extreme wind amounted to unfair competition. In the high-tech world of winter sports, where engineers can design the perfect track, and psychologists can soothe an athlete's nerves, the experts have yet to figure out how to get the weather to play by the rules.

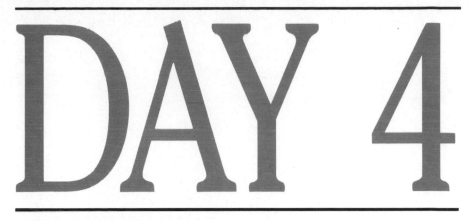

DAY 4

She is a mercurial sweet sixteen; he is a stolid twenty-one years old. Almost twice her weight, he is tall and thickly muscled with impassive features; she has a sylphlike frame and a radiant smile. On a date, they would make an incongruous couple. But on skates, Soviet ice acrobats Ekaterina Gordeeva and Serguei Grinkov were a marvel of harmony. Covering the ice with breathtaking speed and balletic grace, they seemed to move with a single mind—even though he plays the straight man while she is the star. And whether she was twirling in a satellite orbit or pinwheeling upside down on the axis of his arm, that absolutely convincing smile never left her face. For Gordeeva and Grinkov, the free program of figure skating pairs was more a coronation than a contest. When other skaters performed, the tension in the crowd was palpable. Each time the contestants took risks, there was a collective gasp, which turned to a joyous shriek or a sympathetic groan depending on the success or failure. But Gordeeva and Grinkov offered an excitement of a different order. The audience sat back and watched with a sense of awe unfettered by anxiety, because no one expected them to make mistakes. As it turned out, it was hard to detect even the slightest sign of insecurity in their performance, never mind a visible slip. The judges, however, refrained from awarding perfect scores of 6.0; most settled on 5.9. There were still three pairs left to skate. Only the Soviet veterans Elena Valova and Oleg Vassiliev, who took the silver, came close to Gordeeva and Grinkov. Jill Watson and Peter Oppegard of the United States captured the bronze, skating with verve and style to secure their country's first medal in the Games. Meanwhile the Canadians delighted the crowd with some of the most adventurous choreography of the evening—although they failed to charm the judges.

Twirling in midair, Ekaterina Gordeeva hangs suspended above the outstretched arms of her partner, Serguei Grinkov. The Soviets took the gold in the pairs, skating with technical brilliance and assured grace.

Figure Skating

ABOVE:
Despite a fall, Jill Watson and Peter Oppegard won the United States' first medal of the Games. Skating to flamenco rhythms, they took the bronze in the pairs.

It was as if there were two separate events in the pairs long program. There was Gordeeva and Grinkov—and then there was everyone else. To the classical sounds of Chopin and Mendelssohn, the Soviet pair skated with dispassionate perfection in a stratosphere all their own. Meanwhile their more mortal competitors engaged in the high drama that comes with skirting the edge of one's capabilities—and the audience skated with them, balancing on that energy that extends from skate blades to fingertips. The lyrical duet of Valova and Vassiliev of the USSR was full of daring maneuvers and was especially impressive considering that an ankle injury almost denied her the opportunity to compete. Many skaters fell, including Jill Watson, who bounced back up to win a medal. The lunging acrobatics of Canada's Denise Benning, who placed sixth with her partner Lyndon Johnston, took the crowd's breath away.

Then Canadians Christine Hough and Doug Ladret provided a boldly expressive performance, with a finale in which Ladret dropped Hough to the ice in a deliberate parody of a fall. But the evening's boldest departure from tradition came from Canadians Isabelle Brasseur and Lloyd Eisler, whose technically flawed performance—set to a Beatles medley—downshifted through passion, humor, and tenderness. But, to loud boos from the crowd, the judges underlined their distaste for the contemporary by awarding demonstrably mediocre marks in the category of artistic impression.

RIGHT:
Denise Benning and Lyndon Johnston gave a thrilling, risk-filled performance.

Luge

ABOVE:
An American fan at the luge competition.

RIGHT:
Laurence Bonici of France hurtles past the shadows of spectators crowding the luge track. The women's event was dominated by the German Democratic Republic, which took all three medals.

At the halfway point in the women's luge, the German Democratic Republic seemed poised for a repeat medal sweep and a place in Olympic history. Led by European champion Ute Oberhoffner, East Germans captured first, second, and third place in the first round of the women's singles. In 1984 at Sarajevo, East German women took gold, silver, and bronze—no nation has ever swept three luge medals at two successive Olympic games. Canada's Marie Claude Doyon, a twenty-two-year-old contender from Sherbrooke, Quebec, secured sixth place. But her coach, Carole Keyes, said, "It will be very hard to beat the East Germans. The only way I can see it is if one of them makes a mistake."

American luger Bonny Warner, who placed eighth, added some unusual technology to her equipment: a twelve-inch-wide elastic band that she wrapped around her torso to flatten her breasts. "It gives you better aerodynamics," she explained. "We tested it out in a wind tunnel and it makes a difference. But I think it also gives a psychological edge. I'm the only one who uses it."

Alpine Skiing

To the delight of coach Heinz Stohl (below), Canada's Felix Belczyk (above) came in third behind Pirmin Zurbriggen of Switzerland and Franck Piccard of France in the men's combined downhill. Jeff Olson (right) of the United States showed good form on the demanding course but was among six who failed to finish the race.

With the sun shining brightly on Mount Allan, lightning struck for the second time in two days in the form of Swiss skier Pirmin Zurbriggen. The gold-medal winner of the previous day's downhill event mastered a slightly shorter course to win the downhill portion of the combined event—leaving only the next day's slalom run between him and a second gold medal. After Monday's dismal alpine debut, the Canadians found some relief in a third-place finish by Felix Belczyk. And hopes soared for the women's alpine team after Canadians Laurie Graham and Karen Percy tore up the downhill course in training runs. The camaraderie between Graham and Percy, roommates at Nakiska, contrasted with the legendary chill between the two Swiss downhill superstars, Michela Figini and Maria Walliser. "They are as different as night and day," explained Graham. "Canadians are more open-minded and can see the whole picture. Unlike the Swiss, we don't think the whole ski life is lived on the mountain."

Hockey

Marc Habscheid holds back Fredy Luethi of Switzerland in a game that Canada won 4-2.

It was a scrappy, defensive game, in which Team Canada defenseman Tony Stiles scored his second concussion in a week. As Stiles lined up Swiss forward Peter Jaks for a body check, Jaks jumped up, hitting Stiles with his elbow and knee and knocking him out cold: the defenseman spent the night in hospital. Team Canada labored artlessly for much of the game, then finally acquired some offensive acumen in the third period, when Gord Sherven cracked a 1-1 tie with a slapshot drive from inside the blue line. The 4-2 final score put Canada on top of the tournament's A pool with a 2-0 record.

Meanwhile, a plucky Polish squad—which came within a crossbar's width of holding Canada to a tie earlier in the week—surprised even themselves by earning a 1-1 tie with Sweden, the reigning world champions. And Finland atoned for its opening loss to Switzerland with a 10-1 scoring spree against France. The French coach, Kjell Larsson, explained that his team's primary aim in the twelve-team tournament was to learn from the other teams. "Our next goal," he added, "is to finish eleventh." A modest aim indeed.

ABOVE:
The puck seems to hover in the air between
Swiss goalie Richard Bucher, his teammate Felix
Hollenstein, and Canada's Jim Peplinski.

RIGHT:
An airborne Markus Leuenberger of Switzerland
crashes into Ken Yaremchuk of Canada during
a game in which defensive acumen outstripped
excitement.

DAY 5

The finish line — that elusive horizon at the end of a race — can play tricks on the mind. It is a mirage that pulls the athlete through the final paces, drawing out hidden reserves of energy and will. When Sweden's Tomas Gustafson leaned into the final lap of the 5000-metre speed skating event, he was almost a second behind the leading time. A win by Holland's Leendert Visser seemed inevitable. Then suddenly the Swede accelerated. He skated harder and faster than he had ever thought possible as the announcer's voice rose above the crowd's roar: "He's going for the bronze! He's going for the gold!" He went for the gold. Elsewhere that day, on the last leg of a cross-country sprint, Finland's Marjo Matikainen found a final surge of power in her wilting muscles as she poled her way to the finish. Lunging toward the line, she collapsed and swooned forward into the snow, a beatific look of elation and exhaustion passing over her face. After a 5-kilometre sprint, Matikainen had won the gold by a wafer-thin margin of 1.3 seconds. The mirage of victory evaporated for Swiss alpine ace Pirmin Zurbriggen, as he zigzagged through the final gates of the combined slalom. He was skiing beautifully, and all he had to do was complete the race in order to win his second gold medal of the Games. Perhaps his mind was already beyond the finish line when his ski tip strayed a few centimetres toward the gate. Suddenly alpine skiing's brightest star crashed. But then it was a day in which very little went the way it was supposed to. Gusting winds forced the cancellation of the women's luge and the 90-metre ski jump, and critics complained that the facilities on Canada Olympic Park's exposed hillside were built in the wrong place. Yet, while some athletes wondered if they would ever start, others felt as if the strain of competition would never end. "I was so tired," recalled Matikainen. "I just remember there was a finish line, then I can't remember. I saw the red line — and that was enough."

Rudely awakened from his dream of sweeping the alpine events, Pirmin Zurbriggen takes a tumble. His ski caught a gate and he spun out of control during the slalom, the final round of the combined event.

Alpine Skiing

Austrian Hubert Strolz streaks toward a gold medal in the combined event.

The story was not so much who won as who lost. Light snow was falling on the slopes of Mount Allan when Pirmin Zurbriggen pushed off into his slalom run in the final round of the combined alpine event. He was swooping down the course with a fluid, catlike rhythm when, seconds before the finish line, his right ski snared a gate. His skis separated and he flew tumbling off the course. "I don't understand what happened," the Swiss skier said after the race. "I was calm and under control. Everything was going perfectly . . . but suddenly I was on my back." The crash spoiled Zurbriggen's bid for an unprecedented five-medal sweep of the alpine events. And it seemed to have a humbling effect on the soft-spoken star. "Yeah, five medals was a bit much," he conceded. "Perhaps three." France's top-ranked Franck Piccard suffered a

His skis sending up a cloud of snow, Katsuhito Kumagai carves a turn on the slalom course. He finished nineteenth in the race and twenty-first in the combined event—a marriage of downhill and slalom races.

similar crash, allowing Austria to make a one-two punch in the combined event. Hubert Strolz took the gold, and teammate Bernhard Gstrein claimed the silver. Switzerland's Paul Accola captured bronze with two first-place slalom finishes, compensating for a weak showing in the downhill portion of the event.

Figure Skating

Brian Boitano concentrates during compulsories.

To the spectator, compulsory figures are one of the slowest and strangest events in the Olympic repertoire—about as exciting as watching medieval monks transcribing manuscripts. Bereft of spangles and sequins, the world's most-celebrated ice acrobats are reduced to patient draftsmen. Dressed in sweat suits, they drift at a snail's pace, attempting to etch perfect circles into the ice under the close scrutiny of the judges, who line up on the rink beside them like stern sentinels. After each skater completes his design, several judges clear away the shavings and examine the tracings, like detectives dusting for fingerprints. What is most baffling about the event is that it is held in public. Still, compulsory figures represent a venerable tradition in the ice arts, and despite the dearth of public interest, the painstaking exercise accounts for a significant 30 percent of the skater's final score.

In Calgary, the compulsory figures served as a ritual prelude to the drama to follow—the battle of the Brians. Brian Boitano of the United States and Brian Orser of Canada placed second and third, with the disciplined Soviet Alexandre Fadeev in the lead as expected. The exercise also served as a preliminary test for the famous Orser jitters, which were considered the main obstacle between him and a medal. Before entering the arena, Orser walked over to an empty McMahon Stadium, took a seat in the bleachers, and stared at the Olympic flame. "I got inspired," he recalled.

Cross-Country Skiing

Finland's Marjo Matikainen smiles in triumph.

Gold-medal winner Marjo Matikainen of Finland was not the only athlete lying in the snow at the end of the women's cross-country sprint. Angela Schmidt Foster, the most promising contender on the Canadian team, collapsed with exhaustion as she crossed the line. Placing thirty-second in a field of fifty-five skiers, Schmidt Foster admitted she simply wasn't in good enough physical condition to handle the course: "Every hill was tough for me. I just had to keep pushing. When you are at your peak, your body flies up and down the hills. Today I knew by the second hill that I just didn't have it." Subjected to mounting public criticism from her outspoken coach, Marty Hall, she was beginning to feel the strain of Olympic responsibility. "I'm just very sad," she said. "I'm trying to do my best for Canada."

Only the Soviets proved they could consistently survive the rigors of the Canmore course. And while Matikainen robbed them of the gold in the sprint event, the Soviets tightened their grip on Nordic supremacy by capturing silver and bronze.

RIGHT:
Jinfen Wang of the People's Republic of China
found the 5-kilometre cross-country course in
Canmore too grueling and failed to finish. Marjo
Matikainen won the gold by a margin of only
1.3 seconds.

FOLLOWING PAGES:
Against a backdrop of snow-covered mountains,
Karin Jager of the Federal Republic of Germany
strides along the cross-country course. The
5-kilometre race drained the energy of even
the fittest athletes.

Hockey

With sixteen seconds left to play, the Americans thought they had scored a goal against the USSR but the whistle had blown.

The miracle that the Americans were hoping for never materialized. But the team of rambunctious collegians making up Team USA certainly gave the USSR professionals a run for their money. Trying their best to disrupt the Soviets' billiard-ball passing game with aggressive play, the Americans possessed the spirit but lacked the skill. The Soviets took advantage of their defensive weakness to rack up a 6-2 score by the end of the second period. The Americans fought back valiantly in the third until they had pared the Soviet lead to a single goal. But the Cinderella story of the Americans' gold-medal victory against the Soviets in Lake Placid was not to be repeated. After Brian Leetch slapped a shot off the post, the Soviets' defensive wizard, Viatcheslav Fetissov, snuffed out the USA's hopes with his second goal of the night. Earlier in the day, in two decidedly less dramatic contests, Czechoslovakia hammered Norway 10-1, and the Federal Republic of Germany remained unbeaten after defeating Austria 3-1.

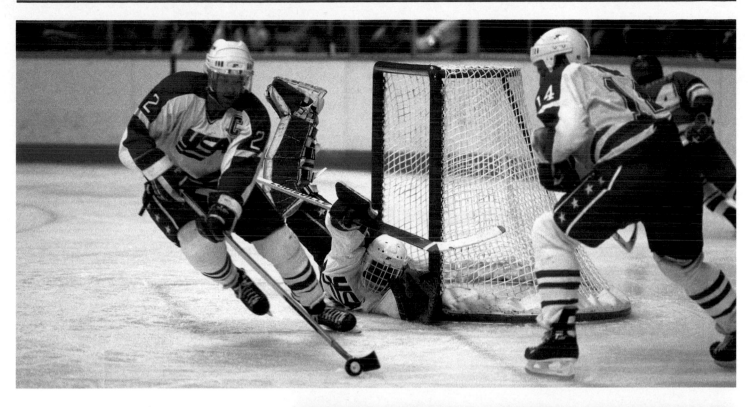

ABOVE:
Brian Leetch picks up the puck after a dramatic
rebound at the U.S. net.

Weak goaltending was a major factor in the U.S.
defeat by the Soviets. Serguei Mylnikov (above)
played a solid game in contrast to the poor
performance of American Chris Terreri (right).

Speed Skating

Once again, the slick ice of the speed skating oval proved that no outdoor record is safe in an indoor rink. In Wednesday's 5000-metres, a total of twenty-nine skaters surpassed the world record set by Eric Heiden at Lake Placid in 1980. But all eyes turned to Tomas Gustafson as he defied the crowd's expectations with an incredible final lap. The skater, who raised both arms in triumph after looking up at his time, later said, "When I saw the score-board—how do you describe happiness? I have to write a poem here." For Gustafson, the defending Olympic champion, the gold medal marked a break in a series of traumas, including the death of his father and a bout with meningitis. Of his last lap, he said, "I don't think I've ever skated a better hundred metres." By contrast, Canadian hopeful Benoit Lamarche, placing twenty-first, dragged himself across the finish line after exhausting his energy too early in the race.

Swedish speed skater Tomas Gustafson gives a victory salute after winning the gold in the 5000-metre race. His time of 6:44.63 broke the Olympic record of 7:02.29 set by American Eric Heiden.

Disabled Skiing

The winners of the disabled skiing competition—second-place Ake Pettersson of Sweden, first-place Hans Anton Aalien of Norway, and third-place Asmund Tveit, also of Norway—wave their victory bouquets from the podium.

It was the most unusual event of the day, and one that seemed to leave all the participants gratified—for having skied in the tracks of the Olympians. None of the athletes could see the colorful banners at the finish line, and each was guided along the course by sighted skiers ahead of them. But they could hear the cheers of the crowd. The fifteen sightless athletes competing in the 5-kilometre cross-country race for the blind were fulfilling a dream. They included a fifty-four-year-old grandmother, Austria's Doris Campbell, who has traveled all over the world to compete in blind Nordic races for the past sixteen years. "It was a harder race than I thought it would be," she said after a spirited finish. Although Campbell didn't win one of the medals in the exhibition, her determination made her an exemplary symbol of the Olympic ideal.

All the contestants in the disabled skiing exhibition are blind. They are led down the course by guides. Here, Hans Anton Aalien, the winner, is guided by A. Homb.

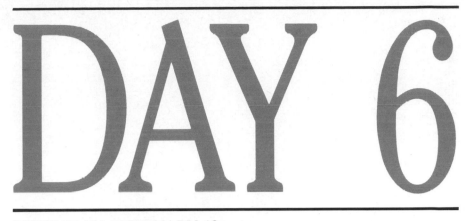

DAY 6

THURSDAY, FEBRUARY 18

A day of disappointment. The troubles started at Nakiska, where an eager crowd awaited the start of the women's downhill. The sky was an immaculate blue, then, just minutes before race time, gray clouds sealed off the sun and the wind picked up. Soon a howling gale was buffeting the gates on Mount Allan's upper slopes, and the race was postponed until the next day—but not before the U.S. team's brightest hope, Pam Fletcher, had been cruelly knocked out of contention. Skiing a warm-up run earlier in the morning, she collided with a course worker and broke her leg. "It was like hitting a tree," recalled Fletcher. At the 90-metre team ski jump, which was also canceled after some delay, a strangely similar accident occurred. While entertaining the restless crowd, one of the forerunners veered off course and hit an ABC cameraman. As the nagging wind rekindled the controversy over the location of Calgary's outdoor sites, the host country endured another setback when Team Canada fell to defeat in a hockey game against Finland. Canadians did find some relief in a mesmerizing display of figure skating by Brian Orser. His unparalleled performance cleared the way for a final showdown with his U.S. rival, Brian Boitano. For Americans, the day offered another sad episode in the saga of U.S. speed skater Dan Jansen. A few days earlier, after learning of his sister's death from leukemia, he fell in the 500-metre race. In the 1000-metre event, he fell again. However, on a day of failed hopes, one athlete emerged to win a niche in Olympic history. Leading a rout of the women's luge by the German Democratic Republic, 1984 gold medalist Steffi Walter became the first singles competitor to retain an Olympic title. And her country became the first to sweep a luge event in two successive Games. As she stood on a podium in Olympic Plaza that evening, her eyes welled with tears. Her flag was raised in triplicate; her anthem was played. And the woman who had made herself into a racing machine was human once again.

The "battle of the Brians" intensifies as Brian Orser of Canada dazzles the crowd to win the short program in the men's figure skating competition.

Figure Skating

The other half of the battle of the Brians, Brian Boitano of the USA, performs with liquid grace to come in second in the short program.

The battle of the Brians, round two—the short program. Each skater executes a series of rapid and complicated maneuvers with exotic names like the camel spin and the death drop. The most difficult move of all—the trick of alchemy that separates gold and silver from the baser metals—is the triple axel followed quickly by the double loop. Coming out of that move, Soviet skater Alexandre Fadeev, the one skater who threatened to make the contest a three-way race, stumbled badly. Both Brian Orser of Canada and Brian Boitano of the United States flew through the two-part maneuver with dazzling precision. But the two skaters possessed radically different styles. In blue glitter, Orser danced and spun to the fast-pumping rhythms of big-band jazz; he cut across the ice with a lighthearted, almost playful attitude. Boitano, striking a formal pose in a black vest and white satin shirt, skated a more dignified program, accompanied by the surging drama of classical ballet music. In the end, it was hard to choose between the two performances, although Orser edged out his rival in the judges' scores. But with his higher standing in compulsory figures, Boitano still led by a faint margin as they headed into the long program's final showdown. There, a victor would finally emerge.

Luge

ABOVE:
In skintight clothing and clawed gloves, the lugers appear more extraterrestrial than Olympic. The top Canadian in the women's luge, Marie Claude Doyon, placed seventh.

RIGHT:
Despite the number of days that spectators have been turned away from Canada Olympic Park because high winds canceled the event, crowds gather once again to watch the women's luge.

She waited. Head bowed, she visualized the run ahead. A long pause. She licked her lips and slid the visor of her helmet over her face. She gripped the red handles at the top of the run. Then Steffi Walter slid back, extending her arms, and pushed herself hard over the brink. Quick, clawed gloves paddled the ice three times. Then Walter leaned back on the sled like an astronaut surrendering to exaggerated gravity. As she rocketed down the chute, controlling her trajectory with expert yet imperceptible movements, you could see the g-forces playing over the blue-sheathed surface of her body. She looked extraterrestrial.

Luge offers the most exotic wardrobe in all Olympic sport. Over various layers of undergarments, Walter wore a weighted vest. Her calves were tied together with garters and a rubber band to keep her toes pointed correctly. Suspenders and cords ran from thighs to helmet to keep her head from snapping back as she slid down the course at 90 kilometres per hour. And on top of it all she wore that airtight plastic speed suit. Steffi Walter's race to glory took less than a minute from top to bottom. But it took a lot longer to get dressed for it.

Hockey

Canadian goalie Sean Burke does the splits to make a save. Although he stopped the puck this time, Canada lost 3-1 in the disappointing game against Finland.

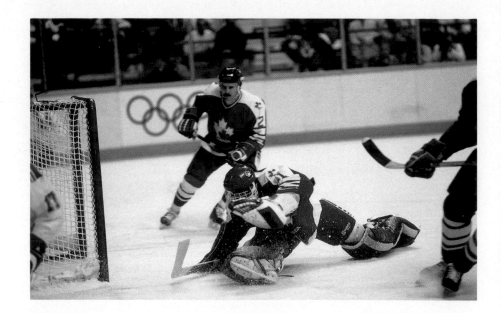

Hockey was becoming the great leveler at the Olympics. Some teams—notably Poland and the Federal Republic of Germany—were displaying more pluck than anyone suspected they possessed. Others, including Canada, were failing to live up to expectations. While Poland walked over France 6-2, and Sweden cruised past Switzerland 4-2, the dire news for hometown fans in the Olympic city was Canada's 3-1 loss to Finland. Frustration with Finn goalie Jarmo Myllys became evident when Team Canada pulled out a bizarre trump card. The Canadians pointed out that Myllys' mask did not meet the mandatory dimensions—the spaces were the wrong size—and the referee dutifully awarded a two-minute penalty against Finland. Team Canada knew about the mask all along. They had just been waiting for the right moment to mention it. They found a hole in Myllys' mask, but they couldn't find the space between him and the net.

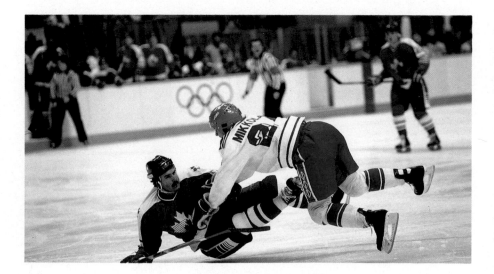

Just before the moment of impact: Reijo Mikkolainen of Finland about to land on Team Canada defenseman Tim Watters.

Speed Skating

ABOVE:
Jens-Uwe Mey of the German Democratic Republic leans into a turn in the men's 1000-metre speed skating event. Although disappointing for North Americans, the event provided the USSR and GDR with medals. Mey took the silver.

BELOW:
Having given his all in the 1000-metre, Gaetan Boucher collapses after the race, unable to reach a bench before removing his skates.

North Americans were rooting for two sentimental favorites in the 1000-metre race: Dan Jansen of the United States and Gaetan Boucher of Canada. Jansen was skating well. On the penultimate straightaway, it looked as if he was on his way to a medal when his skate caught an edge, and his feet slid out from under him. After the race he flew home to Wisconsin by private jet for his sister's funeral, but he planned to return to Calgary to watch his fiancée, Canadian speed skater Natalie Grenier, compete. For his part, Boucher had a fast start and maintained a strong pace until the final lap, when his exhaustion began to show. Rounding the last corner, he wobbled slightly, touching his hand to the ice. Still, he placed fifth. The 1984 gold medalist seemed satisfied with his performance. "Nothing went wrong," he said. "I just don't have the efficiency I used to have." The winner was Soviet Nikolai Gouliaev, who—in the North American media at least—was known as the man who passed a package of steroids to a Norwegian skater a month before the Games.

DAY 7

True, it was just a bronze. But it was the first Winter Olympic medal won by Canada on its own terrain—and the nation's first Olympic alpine medal in eight years. Certainly, the crowd of 50 000 revelers who descended on Calgary's Olympic Plaza that night to greet Karen Percy considered it adequate cause for celebration. A dark horse in the women's downhill, the twenty-one-year-old from Banff was leading early in the race. At the bottom of the run, she watched anxiously as Marina Kiehl of the Federal Republic of Germany knocked her out of first place, then as Switzerland's Brigitte Oertli eclipsed her time by one-hundredth of a second. That infinitesimal margin—equivalent to the time it takes for a mousetrap to spring shut—was enough to separate silver from bronze. But Percy was delighted with the bronze, realizing that an equally narrow margin could have kept her out of the medals altogether. "I'm very, very, very happy," she said. "What more could I ask for?" But the downhill race was a bittersweet triumph for Canada's alpine team. Kellie Casey of Collingwood, Ontario, crashed into the net on the steep upper section of the run, seriously tearing ligaments in her knee. And alpine veteran Laurie Graham, hoping to crown her ten-year career with an Olympic medal, saw her dream dissolve with a fifth-place finish. For a racer who considered herself in "the evening" of her career, the one-second gulf between her and gold meant hundreds of thousands of dollars in lost endorsements. After the race, Graham put on a brave face. "I cannot look back at this day and say, 'I blew it,'" she said. "I feel really fine about it. I'm happy with the way I skied." Yet, even as she smiled, Graham could not hold back tears. "I don't care if you see me cry," she told the crowd of reporters gathered around her. "I've handled the pressure right up to now." And now the pressure was finally off.

"I don't care if you see me cry," Laurie Graham told reporters after she narrowly missed winning a medal in the women's downhill. A World Cup competitor since 1980, she was considered a serious contender for a Canadian gold.

Alpine Skiing

Karen Percy of Banff, Alberta, swoops down Mount Allan toward the finish line—and a bronze medal in women's downhill.

Marina Kiehl was as surprised as everyone else when she learned that her wild flight down Mount Allan was good enough for gold. "I was really out of control at the top," she recalled, "and when I crossed the finish line, I thought I was well outside a medal time." Like the other competitors, she had to fight her way through gusts on the upper slopes. Laurie Graham, who admitted the winds were "borderline," also struggled in the top section. But she made no excuses—unlike Swiss superstar Michela Figini. "The wind bothered me," complained the former Olympic champion. "It isn't fair. If you're beaten by the conditions, it's not your fault. I got my medal in Sarajevo, and I got it in normal weather conditions." Figini placed well back in sixteenth place, while her arch-rival on the Swiss team, Maria Walliser, finished fourth. Both were overtaken by a less celebrated teammate, silver medalist Brigitte Oertli, who had been blown off the course the previous day before the race was canceled. Both Oertli and Kiehl felt the one-day delay helped their nerves. It seemed that Nakiska's fickle wind could blow both ways.

ABOVE:
The Canadian fans at Nakiska got a special treat—a chance to watch Karen Percy capture Canada's first Winter Olympic medal won on home soil.

RIGHT:
The joy of victory—Marina Kiehl of the Federal Republic of Germany savors the moment while holding the small stuffed animal presented to the winners.

Hockey

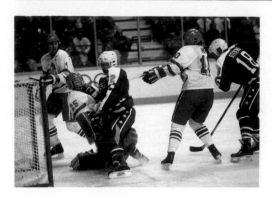

In two games, both of which ended in a 6-3 score, goaltenders had their hands full. In his team's unsuccessful attempt to hold back the USA, Vernon Mott of Norway found himself almost crushed by number two, Brian Leetch (above), and upended in a save on Tony Granato (top right). In the USSR's game with the Federal Republic of Germany, goalie Josef Schlickenrieder (below right) lost his stick stopping a shot by Soviet Serguei Svetlov.

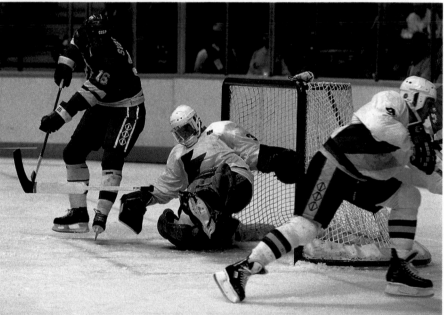

Years ago, coach Xaver Unsinn of the Federal Republic of Germany promised that he would step down as soon as his team defeated the Soviet Union. That may have been a bid to remain behind the bench until his dying breath. On Day Seven, at least, Unsinn came no closer to retirement, as the Soviets staved off a valiant effort by the FRG. The 6-3 victory left the USSR as the only squad among the tournament's twelve teams without a loss or a tie. Adding luster to the Soviets' elite image were fresh reports that before next season Soviet Olympic stars would be playing in the National Hockey League. In less exciting contests, Czechoslovakia beat Austria 4-0, and the USA kept alive its medal hopes with a 6-3 win over winless Norway.

Luge

If North Americans watching luge for the first time thought it was a strange sport, then the final doubles event—featuring two shrink-wrapped athletes sandwiched onto a small sled—seemed even odder. But luge is extremely popular in the German Democratic Republic, and in Calgary, that country firmly sealed its small-sled supremacy with a sweep of the gold medals in all three events. As world champions Joerg Hoffmann and Jochen Pietzsch shot to victory in the doubles, people began to wonder if the GDR team had some secret formula for success, some scientific compound to make their sleds slicker than the opposition's. "We have no secrets," laughed Hoffmann. "Our training is good. We have good coaches. And we have the experience." In fact, his country has dominated luging for twenty years. Sixteen full-time trainers, many of them former world champions, cultivated the team, whose members were drawn from a vast talent pool. And their exhaustive training program reaped an Olympic harvest of three golds, two silvers, and a bronze.

Canadians Andre Benoit and Bob Gasper were disappointed with their tenth-place finish in the doubles event, although it was a Canadian best. After their first run put them within reach of bronze, the medal slipped away as their sled glanced off the wall at the start of the second run.

Joerg Hoffmann and Jochen Pietzsch rocket down the concrete luge track to a first-place finish in doubles. The German Democratic Republic also took the silver in the event.

Curling

On a day when ligaments were shredded and visions of gold vanished on the slopes of Mount Allan, a more subdued exercise took place at the Max Bell Arena in Calgary. Perhaps because its participants were not acrobats, daredevils, or paragons of cardio-vascular virtuosity, they attracted less attention. And perhaps because it is not wise to throw the rocks "swifter, higher, stronger" (in a literal interpretation of the Olympic motto), the medals awaiting the winners would not count in the international tally. But here was a sport in which Canadians seemed to have a definite edge. Lots of people in the German Democratic Republic may live and breathe luge, but 753 000 Canadians slid a rock down a curling rink at least once in 1987. And the fact that Canada's Linda Moore made a game-ending double takeout with her final shot to win curling's semifinal 6-5 against Norway did not escape them.

Cross-Country Skiing

ABOVE:
Mikhail Deviatiarov of the USSR wins the
15-kilometre cross-country.

LEFT:
Jani Krsinar of Yugoslavia catches his breath
after finishing almost halfway back in a field
of eighty-five in the men's 15-kilometre cross-
country event.

While the wind persisted in making itself an issue at other Olympic
venues, the tree-lined trails of Canmore's cross-country courses
presented a different challenge. The steep grades and bumpy
downhill stretches, which allowed skiers to attain speeds of over
80 kilometres per hour, made the courses the toughest and fastest
in Olympic cross-country history. Although the weather was mild
and the course was slow on this day, as the Soviets took both gold
and bronze in the men's 15-kilometre event, Mikhail Deviatiarov
set a new Olympic record for the distance. The Soviets' continued
domination of Sweden's stars puzzled observers until Deviatiarov,
conjuring up a spy-novel scenario, revealed that his team had a
special edge: they trained in the Caucasus Mountains on a course
custom-designed to duplicate Canmore's conditions. "We skied at
the same altitude over a course that had the same profile as this
one," said Deviatiarov. Apparently, even the rustic sport of cross-
country is not immune to the invasion of high tech.

ABOVE:
Canada's best showing in the cross-country event was that of Pierre Harvey of St. Lambert, Quebec. Also a cyclist, he competed in both Summer and Winter Olympics in 1984.

RIGHT:
Dwarfed by the Rocky Mountains, the cross-country course at Canmore, 100 kilometres from Calgary, was built especially for the Olympics, but will be used in the future for other international Nordic events.

DAY 8

At the midway point of the Games, the duel on ice reached its apogee: the final round in the battle of the Brians was about to be fought. The uncanny symmetry of their toy-soldier costumes, each with military epaulets and gold-leaf braid, suggested an epic showdown between two generals: American Brian Boitano in Prussian blue and Canada's Brian Orser in Coldstream crimson. Only one of the two could emerge victorious. And, in the end, only one was flawless. Executing crisp maneuvers to the martial sound-track of Napoleon, *Boitano seemed imbued with the confidence of his music. When he tossed back his head after the final pirouette, it was clear he had given the performance of his life, although the judges' marks still left room at the top for Orser. The arena was full of flag-waving partisans who greeted his arrival with shouts of "Go, Orser, go!" as if he were an entire hometown hockey team. They watched as he tried to shake tension from his muscles in the warm-up. Then they held their breath as he soared into his first letter-perfect leap, boldly landing into a well of silence left by a dramatic pause in the music. But moments later, as he descended from a triple flip, Orser faltered. The error was slight, yet visible enough to send a shudder through the crowd and blunt the edge of his performance. Suddenly conservative, the flamboyant skater pared his final triple axel down to a double. Afterward, there was a flurry of optimism when Orser's marks for artistic impression — including a perfect 6.0 from the Czechoslovakian judge — exceeded Boitano's. But his lower technical score spelled defeat by the finest of margins. Orser could be proud; he had won a silver medal for his country. Yet it was sad to see Canada's leading contender for a gold medal lose. And the quiet news that Canada struck gold in the demonstration sport of women's curling seemed insufficient consolation.*

Silver, gold, and bronze: Brian Orser, Brian Boitano, and Victor Petrenko were the survivors after one of the most fiercely contested battles of the Olympics.

Figure Skating

Resplendent in studs and sequins, Heiko Fischer of the Federal Republic of Germany delights the audience with a streetwise pose.

There *were* other competitors in the men's free skate aside from Orser and Boitano—twenty-two, to be exact. One of the crowd-pleasers was Heiko Fischer from the Federal Republic of Germany, who stalked the ice in a punk costume of studs and leather to the strains of *West Side Story*. Another was Canada's Kurt Browning, who placed sixth in the free skate with an ambitious program that featured a rare attempt at a quadruple toe-loop which was not wholly successful. But the evening's emotional investment went entirely into the anxiously awaited contest between the two Brians.

Displaying a charisma that he lacked in the short program, Boitano took cool command of the ice. His performance tightly choreographed by Canadian Sandra Bezic, he skated with a measured, military style. Next, Alexandre Fadeev's program, marred by a fall, served as a sort of intermission between the two feature attractions. A crowd desperate to relieve its tension seized on the

Brian Orser, in a toy-soldier costume, performs a variation of a Russian split jump. His stirring performance earned him a silver medal—hardly a failure, but not the gold Canadians had pinned their hopes on.

Slavic rhythms of Fadeev's music for an exuberant round of hand-clapping. Then with Orser's appearance, the tension returned. Displaying a style as sinuous as Boitano's was taut, the Canadian skater traded in the jazz dexterity of his short program for the orchestral angst of Shostakovich's *The Bolt*, but he lacked his usual spark. The scores of the two men were painfully close, with Boitano's technique finally prevailing over Orser's artistry. The music of the skater who followed Orser, Elton John's "Funeral for a Friend," served as an ironic epilogue. Finally, with the crowd almost too numb to notice, Victor Petrenko—a lithe eighteen-year-old Soviet dressed like a pink matador—stole the bronze from his mentor Fadeev, proving that in the dead heat of Olympic competition, nothing is sacred.

The flags of Canada, the USA, and the USSR are saluted during the figure skating medal ceremony.

A wistful Brian Orser waves to the crowd.

Alpine Skiing

BELOW:
Austria's Anita Wachter shoots past gate five in the women's combined downhill. She came in third, less than half a second faster than Canada's Michelle McKendry.

FOLLOWING PAGES:
Carole Merle of France virtually flew downhill to a first-place finish.

Encouraged by Karen Percy's bronze medal victory in downhill, the Canadian women's team continued to ski aggressively. In the downhill portion of the women's combined, three Canadians placed in the top ten: Michelle McKendry, Kerrin Lee, and Percy. Swiss star Maria Walliser—still disgruntled after failing to win a medal in the previous day's windblown downhill event—placed second behind France's Carole Merle. Walliser pointed to her standing in the combined downhill as evidence that the main event the day before should have been delayed. She was, however, pessimistic about her chances in the combined event, which is weighted in favor of slalom. "All the slalom specialists will go for the medals," she said.

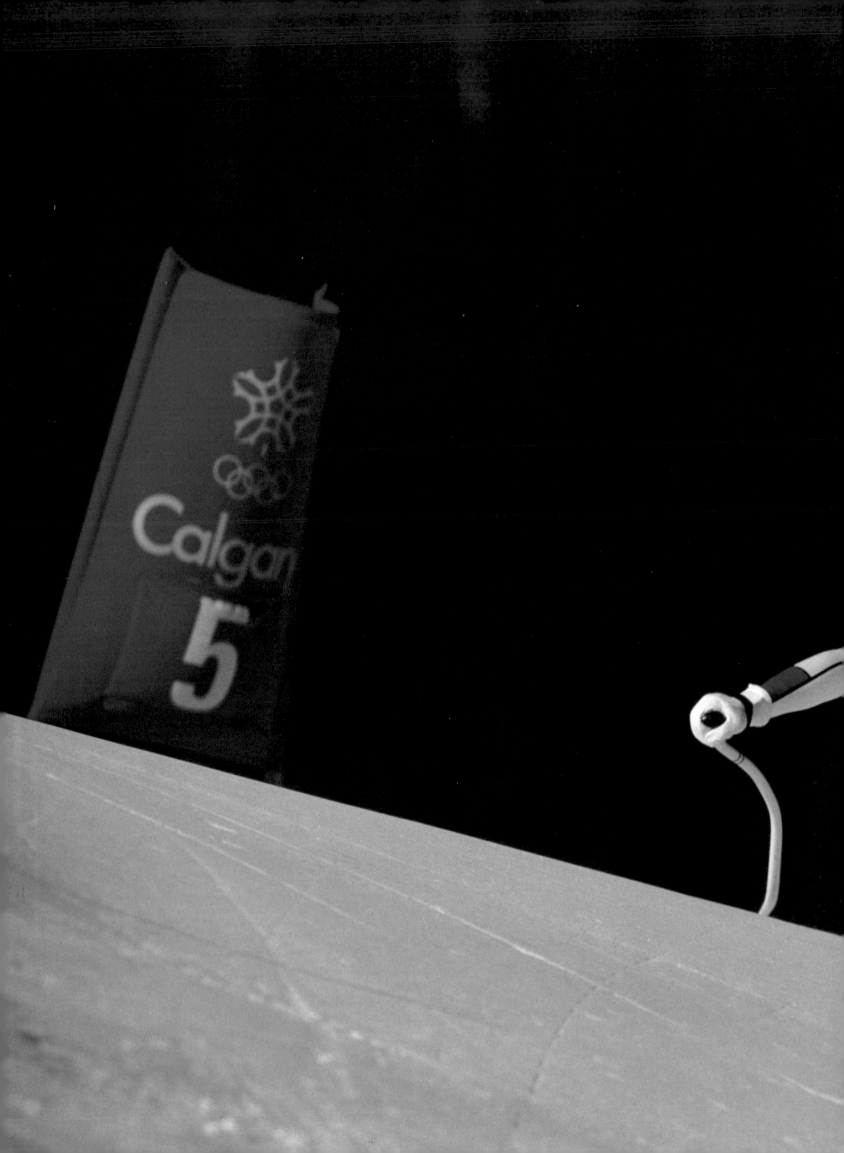

Biathlon

Valeri Medvedtsev of the USSR pushes stren-
uously up a grade on the men's 20-kilometre
biathlon. He completed the course with a time
of 56:54.6 to win the silver medal.

The sport is a peculiar hybrid. One minute the athlete is striding
down a cross-country course with a rifle strapped to his back.
The next, he is trying to relax his breathing and slow his heartbeat
so he can aim the rifle at a bull's-eye. The egg-and-spoon race of
Olympic competition, biathlon requires athletes to maintain an
extraordinary balance between exertion and calm. And, as if the
sport were not tricky enough to begin with, the seventy-one
biathletes competing in Canmore's 20-kilometre individual event
faced strong winds on the target range and wet snow on the trails.
No one hit all twenty targets in the event, but world champion
Frank-Peter Roetsch of the German Democratic Republic made
up the penalty points with fast skiing. "I felt really good," said
Roetsch. "I could have skied another twenty kilometres." Roetsch
took the gold medal, finishing twenty-one seconds ahead of the
Soviet Union's top-ranked biathlete, Valeri Medvedtsev.

Speed Skating

ABOVE:
Speed skater Andre Hoffmann of the German Democratic Republic strides to a gold medal and an Olympic record time in the men's 1500-metres.

RIGHT:
Without looking back, Gaetan Boucher leaves the speed skating rink after his exhausting, all-out effort, the last of his Olympic career.

The race meant more Olympic gold for the German Democratic Republic, as Andre Hoffmann won the 1500-metre speed skating event and set a new world record. But for many of the Canadian fans at the Olympic Oval, it was also the occasion of a fond farewell to an Olympic hero, Gaetan Boucher. After fourteen years and four Olympic medals—including two golds at Sarajevo—Boucher was ready to hang up his skates. Rounding the last Olympic lap of his career, he skated with all his strength while the fans cheered him on. But too soon he was overtaken by exhaustion and finished ninth. "I'm satisfied," he said later. "I didn't make any mistakes. I just felt tired." He understood as well as anyone that speed skating is a young man's game. But at twenty-nine he gave it one last shot. Then Canada's greatest Olympian waved to the crowd and was gone.

Bobsleigh

ABOVE:
Flag-waving fans at the two-man bobsleigh event.

RIGHT:
The newly designed Calgary bobsleigh track features the latest technology, including more than a hundred computer-controlled timing lights that give interval and sectional times along the entire run.

FAR RIGHT:
Canadians David Leuty and Kevin Tyler leap aboard their two-man sled on a springlike day that raised the track's temperatures and the athletes' tempers.

On a day of glaring sunshine and record-high temperatures, some people were beginning to call the Winter Games the Spring Olympics. The chinook gave Calgary's refrigerated bobsleigh track a severe test during the two-man heats. The ice deteriorated over the day, becoming slower for the late-starting competitors.

Canadians Greg Haydenluck and Lloyd Guss were lucky enough to draw the fifth position in a field of forty-one sleds on the opening day of the two-day event. But a number-one start position did not prevent Monaco's Prince Albert from finishing twenty-third. And although the Soviet Union's Ianis Kipours did not push off until twenty-five other sleds had chewed up the track, he won first place. The defending Olympic champion, Wolfgang Hoppe of the German Democratic Republic, tied for second with countryman Bernhard Lehmann. "It's a game of luck," said Hoppe. "It's not only the weather, but the dirt and dust blowing onto the track. It's like running on sandpaper."

Curling

ABOVE:
Three members of Canada's gold-medal-winning curling team, Debbie Jones, Penny Ryan, and Linda Moore.

BELOW:
Swedish skip Elisabeth Hogstrom throws the rock during the women's curling final.

Because curling was a demonstration sport, its medals lacked official value as coin of the Olympic realm. Nevertheless, Vancouver's Linda Moore was thrilled to win gold for Canada in her first Olympic competition, defeating her friend Elisabeth Hogstrom of Sweden 7-5. Having watched the Olympics as a spectacle, she said, "I'd never thought about the participation end, and what it would be like to be in the Olympics. Now I know that simply being here is great. In other championships, winning is the only thing." Moore secured victory without having to throw her last rock, although it was a closely fought match. At the midway point, Hogstrom enjoyed a 4-2 lead. Canada scored two points in the sixth, then slid out of reach in the seventh. Meanwhile, in men's curling, Norway swept past Switzerland to take gold, leaving Canada's Ed Lukowich with the bronze.

Hockey

It was not an encouraging display of talent by Team Canada. There they were, standard-bearers of Canada's national sport, battling the twelfth-ranked French team, whose coach cheerfully admitted that he had expected his team to lose by more than ten goals. As it turned out, they lost 9-5. And four of the Canadian goals were scored during a two-and-a-half-minute blitz in the first period. The rest of the time, the teams fought to a draw. The win clinched Canada a berth in the medal round but gave the country's fans reason to feel anxious. The French, thrilled to have scored so many goals, were delirious in defeat. Meanwhile, the Swiss beat Poland 4-1. And the Swedes tied the Finns 3-3 in a boring defensive duel. Offering his own vision of the Olympic ideal, Swedish captain Thomas Rundqvist explained, "Winning is all that matters; how you do it is not so important."

Sweden's Michael Hjalm shares a happy moment with a teammate. There was less reason for joy after the game, which ended in a 3-3 tie.

DAY 9

A medal is a medal is a medal — but the value of Olympic gold inflates or depreciates according to how it is acquired. It was not unusual to hear an athlete talk about how he or she might have won a medal if blessed with better luck, a more favorable starting position, or more benevolent weather. But on the ninth day of the Games, several athletes who did win medals were questioning the logic of their own triumphs. One was Franck Piccard of France, who captured gold in the men's super giant slalom. The snow was icy, and the gates on the steep upper pitch had been set in an unusually tricky configuration. Piccard was one of the first skiers to race. His patterned ski suit flashing by like a Mondrian painting, he crossed the finish line, then slammed his pole down in disgust. "I felt I'd blown it," he explained later. "I was really angry with myself." But while he waited at the bottom, one top-ranked racer after another either skidded off the course or wasted too much time negotiating it. Pirmin Zurbriggen, Alberto Tomba, Marc Girardelli . . . one by one, they dropped from contention, and Piccard became France's first alpine gold medalist since Jean-Claude Killy in 1968. But he sounded less than elated: "To be an Olympic champion in such a race is frustrating because so many people went down." Later, Swiss Maria Walliser seemed equally nonplussed after taking the bronze in the women's combined event. "It's an absolutely unexpected medal," said Walliser. "I skied the combination only to get training for the Super G." At the speed skating Olympic Oval, however, Tomas Gustafson's delight in winning his second gold medal of the Games was unequivocal. Fulfilling a promise he had made to himself after his first medal win, the convivial Swede came up with a poem: "Some say we have to sweat. But, oh, they must forget how nice it is to lay in the sun. Oh, I want to have some fun."

Following in the tracks of countryman Jean-Claude Killy, Franck Piccard heads for a gold medal in the super giant slalom, a new Olympic event, which requires the athlete to make speed turns for the whole length of the course.

Alpine Skiing

ABOVE:
A Cypriot visitor lends an exotic touch to the Winter Games.

BELOW:
Swedish skiers had some of the most whimsical costumes—a superhero outfit for the Super G.

It was billed as a duel between Switzerland's shy golden boy, Pirmin Zurbriggen, and Italy's flamboyant ace, Alberto "La Bomba" Tomba. But no showdown materialized. The super giant slalom— a cross between the giant slalom's technicality and downhill's speed —is an awkward compromise at the best of times. But on this day an unusually tricky course decimated the field of contenders at Nakiska: out of ninety-four athletes who started the race, thirty-seven failed to finish it. The ultimate irony was that Tomba's Italian coach, Tino Pietrogiovanna, drew the right to set the gates. With Tomba's technical style in mind, he made the route extremely difficult—so difficult, in fact, that it proved too much even for Tomba. Rounding the third gate of the course that became known as "Tino's Twister," the Italian skier careened out of control, spun through an ungainly pirouette, then retired from the race. Zurbriggen, skiing fluidly but not fast enough, finished well under par at fifth. That left the race open to an upset, with skiers from France, Austria, and Sweden shutting out the Swiss favorites. Sweden's Lars Borje Eriksson, who flew down the mountain in a yellow Spiderman suit, was certainly surprised to win bronze. And Canada's Jim Read, brother of former downhill champion Ken Read, placed a respectable thirteenth.

ABOVE:
To see and be seen—a fan at Nakiska.

In the final slalom round of the women's combined event, Maria Walliser played tit for tat with Canada's Karen Percy. After being edged out of the downhill medals by Percy the previous week, Walliser traded places with her in the combined. Percy, her appetite whetted by her first taste of Olympic glory, punched through the course with confidence. But one of her poles slipped from her hand as she headed into the final series of slalom gates, upsetting her rhythm enough to drop her into fourth place. "I'm a little upset," said Percy. "A medal was definitely in my reach."

RIGHT:
Brigitte Oertli of Switzerland came in second in the women's combined, ahead of teammate Maria Walliser, who in turn edged Karen Percy into fourth place.

Cross-Country Skiing

Women cross-country skiers tackle an uphill stretch in the 4-x-5-kilometre relay.

While the Soviet Union expanded its cross-country hegemony with a gold medal victory in the women's relay, the athletes and coaches of the Canadian team wondered what had gone wrong. Just a year earlier, the team won a silver medal at the World Cup relay in Canmore; in the Olympic event they placed ninth. The race started badly for the Canadians as lead skier Angela Schmidt Foster got her ski tangled with Carol Gibson's at the relay point. With their morale eroded by poor results in the opening events, the Canadian team seemed overwhelmed by fatigue. "I've never been so dead in ages," said Schmidt Foster after finishing her leg. "I'm too dead to know what it feels like."

The Soviet Union won its sixth gold medal with a first-place finish in cross-country.

FOLLOWING PAGES:
The wind snaps flags and sends snow swirling at Canmore, site of the cross-country events.

Speed Skating

The sweetness of victory and the agony of defeat: both extremes were evident at the Olympic Oval as another world record was eclipsed. Becoming the first Olympian to win double gold in Calgary, Sweden's Tomas Gustafson powered his way to a new record in the 10 000-metre event, completing the grueling twenty-five laps in 13:48.20. "I went on the offense today right from the start," said the twenty-eight-year-old skater. "With one lap to go, I was extremely tired. I didn't think I could reach the record. But I sure tried—and it's a tremendous feeling to see the scoreboard." The race, however, spelled disaster for two top medal contenders. The Swede's arch-rival, Norwegian Geir Karlstad, the former world record holder, went sprawling across the ice with seven laps to go, an accident that shocked the skater as much as the crowd: he said the last time he fell skating was at the age of eleven. And Dutch skater Gerard Kemkers, who took bronze in the 5000-metres, also took a tumble. "The first thing I knew," he said, "I was sitting on the ice. And that's not the way it's supposed to be."

Speed skaters minimize air resistance by wearing skintight hooded suits and crouching low, a posture that also maximizes force. Here, Frode Syyertsen of Norway flashes past.

Leendert Visser of the Netherlands prepares himself before the 10 000-metre race. He came in third, behind Tomas Gustafson, who broke yct another record for his gold.

Hockey

Czech goalie Jaromir Sindel and Soviet player
Alexandre Moguilny dive to the ice.

The Miracle on Ice was not to be. A decisive 4-1 defeat at the
hands of the Federal Republic of Germany put an end to a linger-
ing American dream that there might be a replay of the 1980
euphoria at Lake Placid. Olympic tie-breaking procedures meant
that Team USA had to beat the FRG squad by two goals to advance
to the medal round. But the European team was in an indomitable
mood. Drawing the Americans out of their own zone, they racked
up a 3-0 lead. Goaltender Karl Friesen, one of five Canadian
expatriates playing for the FRG team, repeatedly thwarted the
Americans' offense. The U.S. team did not find the net until third
period; by then it was too late.

Earlier in the day, the Soviets extended their unbeaten streak
by bombarding Czechoslovakia 6-1, prompting Czech coach Jan
Starsi to issue an ominous warning: "If the Russian team continues
to play the way they did tonight, then I don't think they'll find a
worthy opponent in this tournament."

Figure Skating

An ice dancing duo makes elegance an exact science. And in the compulsory figures program, the first round of the Games' three-event ice dancing competition, the emphasis was on footwork. To prescribed rhythms, each pair danced through a series of official steps—the kilian, the paso doble, and the Viennese waltz—in preordained routes around the rink. The judges' results, worth 30 percent of the final mark, mirrored the sport's established world order. Soviet skaters Natalia Bestemianova and Andrei Boukine placed first; their teammates Marina Klimova and Serguei Ponomarenko came second; and Canada's Tracy Wilson and Rob McCall ranked third. McCall compared the three-tiered contest to a hockey game: "There are three periods, and this is the first. We just can't be the Toronto Maple Leafs, that's all."

Freestyle Skiing

Freestyle aerials are nothing if not spectacular. Essentially, they are akin to the tricks a high diver performs, although snow offers a harder landing pad than water does. The previous week, in fact, U.S. freestylist Chris Haslock suffered a concussion after coming down on his back instead of his skis during a training session at Canada Olympic Park. The fall looked much more serious than it was, said Haslock, adding, "It's something that doesn't happen too often." Yet it happened again on this day at the women's freestyle aerials competition when U.S. skier Maria Quintana escaped with a mild concussion after a triple jump ended in a crash.

Disabled Skiing

Calgary's unstable climate became a major participant in the outdoor events at the Winter Games, and disabled skiing was no exception. At Canada Olympic Park—where blowing sand cut short the two-man bobsleigh event—competitors in the giant slalom exhibition for above-the-knee amputees had to cope with melting snow. "It was as if somebody had put a blow-dryer on the course," complained Canadian skier Phil Chew. The top Canadian competitor was Lynda Chyzyk, who had won the slalom gold medal at Innsbruck's World Paralympic Games just one month earlier. In Calgary, in the giant slalom, she placed fourth, after the wrong choice of wax slowed her skis in the opening round.

DAY 10

Some ran in packs; others competed in pairs; and then there were those who raced alone against the clock. In the men's cross-country relay, a herd of skiers poled frantically from a simultaneous start. Funneling into a narrow track, they threaded their way through the forest in shifts, until forty kilometres later the last Swede beat the last Soviet by a matter of seconds, restoring some Nordic pride to a nation that was getting anxious about its cross-country stars. Elsewhere, in the Olympic debut of the dangerous game called short track speed skating, a greyhound gang of racers tacked into centrifugal force on a small, tight-cornered oval. And at the much larger Olympic Oval, diminutive Bonnie Blair became an instant American heroine after streaking from zero to gold in roughly thirty-nine seconds. But for Canadians the woman of the hour was Karen Percy, the blond whiz kid from Banff who skied to her second bronze medal of the Games and was proclaimed Canada's new alpine queen. It was not a fate she had expected as she entered her first Olympics in the shadow of veteran Laurie Graham — but she had certainly prepared for it. She spent the summer hiking up and down Nakiska's Mount Allan, memorizing its contours. From the moment she bolted out of the starting gate of the mountain's Super G course, she was at home. She was the last of the top-ranked skiers to race, and she knew how fast she had to go. She made a couple of mistakes, cutting low through gates near the top, but she caught up as she flexed through turns in a racing tuck, shaving split seconds off the corners. When it was over, she smiled in the Nakiska sun and mused over her fate: "Bronze," she sighed. "It would have been nicer to get a different color, but it's still a medal and I'm really happy."

Thousands cheer as Karen Percy displays her second medal at Olympic Plaza in downtown Calgary.

Alpine Skiing

FAR RIGHT:
Switzerland's Michela Figini, who placed second in the Super G, fulfilled her expectation of taking home an Olympic medal.

Traditionally the Austrians and Swiss have been the arch-rivals of alpine skiing. And after humiliating defeats in the 1984 Olympics and the 1987 world championships, the Austrians were ready for revenge. Their first coup came with Hubert Strolz's gold medal in the combined alpine event the first week of the Games. In the second week, the Austrians struck gold again as Sigrid Wolf won the Super G by a clear margin over Switzerland's Michela Figini and Maria Walliser—with Canadian Karen Percy winning the bronze for the second time in four days. After a poor downhill showing, Figini redeemed herself with a silver medal.

When Wolf suited up for the event, she included a peculiar good-luck charm in her equipment. It was a safety pin that she had kept as a souvenir from an unpleasant experience at a World Cup Super G race six weeks earlier in her home valley of Lech in the Austrian Tirol. She placed first in that race but victory was snatched away when officials disqualified her result because she had used a safety pin to hold her start-number bib in place. They claimed it offered an unfair aerodynamic advantage. For the Olympic Super G, Wolf drew the same start number as she had in Lech. And she wore the same safety pin—but this time it was around her neck.

BELOW:
Skiing aggressively, Karen Percy wins the bronze for the second time in four days.

Hockey

ABOVE:
Canadian fans get across their message of support.

BELOW:
Canada's Randy Gregg holds back Sweden's Michael Hjalm, crushing Sean Burke.

While Karen Percy won her second bronze at Nakiska, Team Canada's hopes for gold dimmed in a hard-fought but frustrating game against Sweden that ended in a 2-2 stalemate. It was a game of heavy traffic along the boards, with plenty of hooking and holding on both sides, although only a single penalty was called. The Canadian offense, lackluster in previous games, assaulted the Swedish net with new energy. Sweden, the reigning world champions, scored first with a slapshot that rocketed from the point. Then Canada's Merlin Malinowski scored a pretty goal after skating through the defense, and Serge Boisvert added another to put Canada ahead 2-1. Sweden tied the score with a fluky goal as Jens Ohling dribbled the puck past the post.

Elsewhere the same day, Finland walked over Poland 5-1, and France's winless record remained unmarred after a 9-0 loss to Switzerland.

Sean Burke's desperate save was not enough to salvage the game for Canada. The final score, a 2-2 tie, left Team Canada in a precarious position going into the medal round.

Speed Skating

U.S. speed skater Bonnie Blair with silver and bronze medalists Christa Rothenburger and Karin Kania of the German Democratic Republic.

When the women speed skaters made their debut at the Olympic Oval, the crux of the contest was the long-awaited showdown between Christa Rothenburger of the German Democratic Republic and Bonnie Blair of the USA. A 500-metre sprint, the race was over very quickly. Rothenburger skated well, breaking her own world record with a time of 39.12 seconds. Then a few minutes later Bonnie Blair's lithe 130 pounds—sheathed in skintight gray and orange stripes—flashed around the oval two-hundredths of a second faster. "In speed skating," said Blair afterward, "any woman's dream is to beat East Germany. For so long they've been on top."

Bobsleigh

FOLLOWING PAGES.
The New Zealand bobsleigh team of Alexander Peterson and Peter Henry, both residents of Calgary, rockets down the track in an event marred by disputes over racing conditions.

Bobsleigh, that adult midway ride through tunnels of ice, was one of the most controversial events of the Winter Games. On Sunday the final heat of the two-man event was postponed when blowing sand made the track too gritty for racing. On Monday the runs were again delayed while race officials waited for the wind to drop and the chute to be repaired. When the race finally resumed, the ice was faster than it had been for the early runs. A sled piloted by the Soviet Union's Ianis Kipours thundered down the track to an upset victory over Wolfgang Hoppe, the German Democratic Republic's world champion. Later, Hoppe, along with a number of top drivers, disputed the fairness of the race. "There were large chunks of ice in the track," he said. "It is very damaged." And FRG driver Anton Fischer bitterly complained, "The whole thing is ridiculous. This has nothing to do with the Olympics. The best thing to do would be to blow up this track."

Figure Skating

Call it Last Tango in Calgary—a tango that lasted, and lasted. For an evening, the Saddledome became a huge Hernando's Hideaway, a white-floored ballroom rattling with castanets, as twenty couples took turns creating fantasies on ice. The skaters were free to dance to whatever music they liked . . . as long as it was a tango. The rules for the original set pattern, the second round in the Olympic ice dancing competition, were strict. But that did not prevent

Soviet skating champions Natalia Bestemianova and Andrei Boukine maintain their lead on the second day of ice dancing competition with a spicy tango performance.

dancers from finding loopholes of creativity within an austere form. There were romantic tangos, sultry tangos, sexy tangos, strutting tangos full of mockery, silky tangos ripe with tenderness. There were tangos that snapped dancers together with slingshot violence, and soft, slithery tangos of entwined limbs.

A Canadian brother and sister dancing for France turned out to be one of the most eye-catching couples. Isabelle and Paul Duchesnay of Aylmer, Quebec, appeared as a gangster and his moll, he with heavy makeup and pomaded hair, she in a black dress slit to the waist. Their staccato parody of the genre was warmly received by the crowd, but it threw the judges into disarray; on a six-point scale, their marks ranged from a 5.1 from the Soviet judge to a 5.8 from his American colleague. The top standings repeated the ranking for compulsory figures. Placing first were Soviet world champions Natalia Bestemianova and Andrei Boukine, who danced passionately to swooping rhythms, followed by teammates Marina Klimova and Serguei Ponomarenko. Canadians Tracy Wilson and Rob McCall came third, dancing fluidly to a tango that was more delicate and soft-edged than the others.

LOWER LEFT:
Canada's ice dancing favorites Tracy Wilson and Rob McCall present a graceful tango to place third in the original set pattern event.

LOWER RIGHT:
Representing France, Quebec natives Isabelle and Paul Duchesnay stunned the audience with their lusty performance.

Cross-Country Skiing

ABOVE:
A herd of cross-country skiers pole strongly on the first leg of the 4-x-10-kilometre relay. The Swedish team (wearing number one) won the race.

BELOW:
Pierre Harvey, a member of the Canadian cross-country relay team, had one of the fastest times of the day. Canada placed ninth in the race.

The men's 4-x-10-kilometre cross-country relay laid to rest any notion that Nordic skiing is a leisurely jaunt through the woods. The race became a pitched battle between the Soviets, who had already won eleven medals at Canmore, and the Swedes, who were trying to regain their reputation as a Nordic power. The turning point of the race occurred in the third leg, when Sweden's Gunde Svan clocked the day's fastest time and overtook Soviet Mikhail Deviatiarov on a downhill glide. Struggling to catch up, Deviatiarov fell as he rounded an icy corner, losing valuable seconds. Breathing hard, the next Soviet skier came close to closing the gap but he, too, went down in the final stretch. Completing the full forty kilometres thirteen seconds ahead of the Soviets, the Swedes took gold in the event—their first cross-country medal at the Games.

Freestyle Skiing

As if mountains were not enough, man had to invent moguls. These diabolical bumps evolve as mounds of snow carved out by skiers on a crowded slope. To the inexperienced skier, they look as intimidating as a storm-tossed sea. To the expert, they provide variety and intrigue, a three-dimensional slalom course. A demonstration event in the freestyle category, mogul skiing is judged on a combination of speed, style, and technique. To the casual observer at Mount Allan, the participants appeared to be going through a nightmare of accelerated deep knee-bends as they bobbed and chopped their way down the course. Although mogul skiing developed on the heavily skied runs of North America, the U.S. favorites, Nelson Carmichael and Steve Desovich, never made it to the medal podium. Bouncing their way to gold were Sweden's Hakan Hansson in men's moguls and Tatjana Mittermayer of the Federal Republic of Germany in women's moguls.

Judged on a combination of speed, style, and technique, mogul freestyle is an exciting skiing event that may become a full-fledged Olympic competition by 1992. Here, Eric Berthon from France performs.

Short Track Speed Skating

LEFT:
Steve Desovich from the USA comes in for a landing. Although a medal favorite, he placed a disappointing fifth in the mogul freestyle.

ABOVE.
Hakan Hansson of Sweden was the surprise winner in the mogul part of the men's freestyle competition.

Participants in the sport don't like to hear it called "roller derby on ice." But to those watching short track speed skating, the analogy is unavoidable. While long track skaters race in pairs around a 400-metre oval with relatively gentle turns, short track competitors race in a pack on a 111-metre oval laid out on a hockey rink. Protected by helmets, gloves, and shin pads, they take the turns at severe angles, often grazing the ice with their left hand to maintain balance. One fall can bring down the whole pack like dominoes, and serious injuries such as severed tendons are not uncommon. As short track made its debut as a demonstration event in Calgary, a dozen skaters fell during the twenty-one races, including two who were taken to hospital. Ki Hoon Kim, a twenty-year-old Korean from Seoul, took the gold medal in the men's 1500-metres. One stride behind was Canada's Louis Grenier, who took silver.

DAY 11

At last, the chinook's spell lifted. The wind eased off, the temperature dropped back to a sane winter level, and the sky came into crisp focus. The cartoon colors of the hot-air-balloon fleet dotted the city's horizon. And at Canada Olympic Park, a record crowd of 80 000 gathered to watch men fly through the air in one of the most serene rites of the Games. That morning Matti Nykanen, the baby-faced wunderkind known as the Flying Finn, rode a glass-walled elevator up a concrete tower to the top of the 90-metre ski jump. To the west he could see the white edge of the distant Rockies; to the east lay Calgary's skyline and beyond it the dun-colored prairie. Putting on his helmet and skis, Nykanen sat on the narrow start bench and gazed down the ramp. He admitted later that he felt a twinge of fear, wondering if the start was positioned too high for his own safety. To beat his competition he would have to jump well past the point where the hill begins to flatten out and landing becomes dangerous. Nykanen bent down and touched the back of his bindings, perhaps to make sure they were still there. He paused, then let go. When he lifted from his crouch near the lip of the ramp, he was moving at about a hundred kilometres per hour. Airborne, he seemed to stretch time, his left arm shifting in his slipstream like a rudder. His skis finally thumped on the snow at the 118.5-metre mark, and Nykanen sailed into Olympic history as the first jumper to win two gold medals at the same Games and the first to strike gold in two successive Olympics. That evening Canadians celebrated as a very different form of grace under pressure thrilled a crowd in the Saddledome. Capturing a bronze medal with a stunning display of ragtime skating, Canadian ice dancers Tracy Wilson and Rob McCall—like the Flying Finn—showed that artistry and athletics were two sides of the same Olympic coin.

Hot-air balloons rising over the city of Calgary provided a colorful and unexpected early-morning treat.

Ski Jumping

Matti Nykanen's headlong flight into Olympic history was the highlight of the 90-metre ski jump. But the crowd found two other competitors almost as exciting. One was Canada's Horst Bulau, who glided an impressive 112.5 metres in his first jump. Bulau lost the chance for a medal when his second jump fell short at 99.5 metres, but his seventh-place result was the best ever achieved by a Canadian jumper at the Olympics. The other attraction, of course, was British jumper Eddy "The Eagle" Edwards, whose fame had soared steadily, even during the days jumping was canceled. There had been some dispute as to whether Edwards would be allowed to jump. It was argued that the odds were too great that he would break his arms and legs in the 90-metre event, especially if the day was windy. But the Eagle, so proud of his last-place jump in the 70-metre event, wanted to go for broke. Pink goggles clamped over his wire-rimmed spectacles, Edwards set his jaw and schussed down the ramp. He lifted off with a tentative jerk, then plopped to a shaky landing 71 metres later. A meagre result but enough to set a new British record.

Edwards' dubious feat became the focus for an interesting debate at the Games. "The Eagle drops out of the sky, he doesn't jump," deadpanned Rob McCormack, chief of competition for ski jumping, who welcomed the publicity Edwards had brought the sport despite his own "mixed feelings." An unamused Norwegian jumping official, Torbjorn Yggeseth, said, "We have thousands of Eddy Edwards in Norway but we never let them jump." Nykanen, however, had the last word: "I do not mind that Eddy jumps," he allowed. "Every sport needs its clowns."

Horst Bulau's seventh-place finish in the 90-metre jump was the best Olympic result ever for a Canadian ski jumper.

Figure Skating

Soviet gold medalists Natalia Bestemianova and Andrei Boukine ease through a dynamic free skate program to complete a triumphant sweep of all three ice dance events.

Ice dancing lacks the acrobatic spins and jumps of pairs skating. In fact, the rules actually forbid a male skater to raise his arms above his shoulders when lifting his partner. But there was no lack of theatrics in ice dancing's final free skate event.

Tracy Wilson and Rob McCall captivated the crowd and captured bronze—Canada's first Olympic ice dance medal—with lightning footwork set to ragtime rhythms. Swooping and sprinting across the ice, they performed an intricate choreography that ballerina Vanessa Harwood, former principal dancer of the National Ballet of Canada, helped create.

Canadian ice dancers Tracy Wilson and Rob McCall clinch their bronze medal with a jazzy free skate routine.

As expected, Soviet veterans Andrei Boukine and Natalia Bestemianova took first place after their tempestuous performance to classical music. The gold complemented the silver they won at Sarajevo, where gold medalists Jayne Torvill and Christopher Dean of Great Britain turned ice dancing's conventions inside out with their expressive impression of *Bolero.* And Marina Klimova and Serguei Ponomarenko, also of the Soviet Union, graduated from Sarajevo bronze to Calgary silver with a delicate dance set to an orchestral medley of Beatles music.

The evening's most provocative skaters were Canadians Isabelle and Paul Duchesnay, dancing for France. Costumed as primitives in tawny velvet, they prowled the ice to the urgent beat of African drums. Their program—a far cry from their gangster-moll routine of the previous evening—was choreographed by ex-Olympian Christopher Dean. But, once again, they seduced the audience only to perplex the judges, whose erratic marks ranged from 5.0 to 5.8. The event, in fact, provoked renewed controversy about judging: after three days, from the first compulsory figures to the final free skate, only two of the twenty couples changed places in the overall standings.

FAR RIGHT:
Tracy Wilson steals a glimpse at the competition while waiting her turn to perform in the free skate event.

Biathlon

Frank-Peter Roetsch had a sound sleep, woke up to a hearty breakfast of bacon and eggs, then prepared his skis for the race. Having already won a gold medal in the 10-kilometre biathlon, he didn't feel pressured to repeat his accomplishment. But that is exactly what he did. Becoming the first double-gold champion in the brief history of Olympic biathlon, Roetsch raced to victory in the 20-kilometre race. His speed on the cross-country track compensated for his lack of accuracy on the target range, as he surpassed another Olympic record. In fact, the Canmore track was so slick that sixty-two of the seventy-two athletes who finished covered the twenty kilometres more quickly than in any previous Olympics. As Roetsch's rival, Soviet Valeri Medvedtsev, won silver, the stage was set for Friday's showdown between the Soviet Union and the German Democratic Republic in biathlon's team relay.

Peter Angerer of the Federal Republic of Germany placed tenth in the 10-kilometre biathlon. The skiing portion of the event is a test of endurance while the shooting portion measures precision.

Pieralberto Carrara of Italy loads his rifle during the 10-kilometre biathlon. If athletes miss the target, they must ski penalty laps.

Speed Skating

Between them, they had won ten Olympic medals and they both hailed from the German Democratic Republic. At Calgary, Karin Kania and Andrea Ehrig found themselves pitted against each other in the same heat of the 3000-metre race. When it was over, both skaters had lost a piece of a dream. Kania, who won a bronze in the 500-metres, had hoped to win five medals of various sorts at the speed skating oval. But she started too fast and couldn't keep up the pace. Her rival, Ehrig, won the heat but lost her bid for a second gold medal in the event when Holland's Yvonne van Gennip streaked across the finish line in a separate heat one-fifteenth of a second faster. "My technical movements are very, very strong," explained van Gennip. "Better than the East Germans'. In the last three or four years, I've always looked up at them, and I was always beaten before I started."

Yvonne van Gennip of Holland skated a perfectly paced 3000-metre race in 4:11.94, setting a new world record and capturing the gold medal.

Nordic Combined

FAR RIGHT:
Todd Wilson of the USA performs to an overflow crowd in the 70-metre ski jump of the team nordic combined.

The change of weather that finally allowed ski jumping to resume also allowed the nordic combined team competition, an inaugural sport at the Olympics, to proceed on schedule. In this event, countries compete first in ski jumping, then in cross-country skiing. And the first stage of the event held a surprise in store for the 40 000 spectators gathered beneath the 70-metre ski jump at Canada Olympic Park. Klaus Sulzenbacher, a twenty-three-year-old Austrian soldier, soared 91 metres —past the 89.5-metre mark set the previous week on the same jump by Finnish ski-jump king, Matti Nykanen. But the Federal Republic of Germany's jumpers achieved better results as a team and took first place in the initial round of the nordic combined, with Austria second and Norway third.

Short Track Speed Skating

Short track speed skating made its Olympic debut as a demonstration event at these Games. This fast-paced competition takes place on a 111-metre oval track in a hockey rink.

Canada's Sylvie Daigle accomplished something in short track skating that eluded her at two previous Olympics on the bigger ovals of conventional speed skating: she won a gold medal. But because the 1500-metre race on the short track was only a demonstration event, her medal—like Canada's gold medal in curling—did not count on the nation's Olympic scorecard. In short track's 500-metre sprint, another Canadian, Mario Vincent, took the silver, and he did not seem bothered by the sport's second-class status. "The only difference," he said, "is in the word *demonstration* on the medal."

Freestyle Skiing

Although it was just a demonstration event, few sports offered anything to match the pyrotechnical grace of freestyle aerial skiing. Some 40 000 spectators at Canada Olympic Park thrilled to the spectacle of skiers jumping into the jurisdiction of high-divers and trampoline artists. And the Canadians in the crowd had the pleasure of seeing a team known as the "Quebec Air Force" outmaneuver the competition to win both gold and bronze medals. Flying ace Jean Marc Rozon placed first after flying off the ramp and executing three turns and four twists in a span of three and a half seconds. "I was surprised," he admitted afterward. "I'd practiced it so many times on the diving board and the trampoline. I said to myself: 'Just do it, just think about the jump and do it.'"

Canada's Jean Marc Rozon, having overcome a serious back injury, won a gold medal in the men's aerials event.

Competitors in the freestyle aerials must perform two different acrobatic jumps as part of their program.

DAY 12

At a party there usually comes a time when the hosts realize they are not having as much fun as the guests. It was that kind of day for Canada, a day when the nation's proprietorial sense of identity with the sport of hockey was rudely violated, as the Soviet Union methodically stripped Team Canada of its chances for a gold or silver medal. It was not the first time, and it will not be the last, but the knowledge that history was repeating itself served as cold comfort. The morning began calmly enough, as skaters moving in surgical slow motion cut compulsory figures into the ice—an ethereal scene compared to the hockey game at the end of the day. People came to watch the compulsory figures program not because it was exciting but because it was a significant prelude to a high drama— and a chance to observe the main protagonists, Debi Thomas and Katarina Witt, in the flesh. Meanwhile, on the other side of town, the irrepressible Matti Nykanen again made winning gold look easy as he led the Finns to victory in the 90-metre team ski jump. Becoming the only jumper in Olympic history to win three gold medals at a single Games, the Flying Finn embraced the honor with his usual nonchalance; allowing himself a smile, he said he might even celebrate. And that night the Finnish team basked in glory on the podium at Olympic Plaza—four young athletes with ice-blue eyes and matching parkas—while Team Canada faced off against the Soviets. Canadians can accept being out-jumped by Finns, out-luged by East Germans, and even out-skied by the Swiss. But Canadians have never gotten used to being humiliated in hockey. The 5-0 game was not a pretty one. It was a clutch-and-grab contest in which the Soviets wore down the Canadians in the first period, stung them hard in the second, then toyed with them in the third. As the Saddledome's raucous crowd sank into morgue-like silence, it was clear that on this night the party was a bust.

The Soviet hockey team's victory crushed Canada's hope for an Olympic gold in a sport the nation considers its own.

Hockey

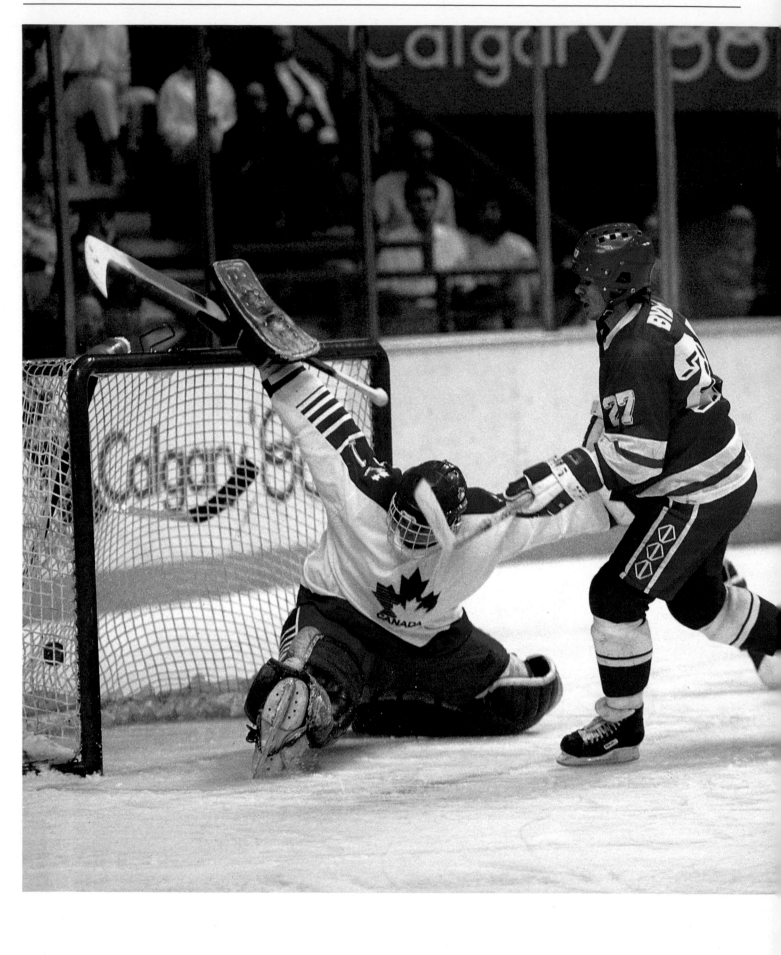

BELOW:
A lethal blow for Team Canada: Viatcheslav Bykov's power-play goal against Sean Burke early in the second period. Tony Stiles, on the right, who had lost his stick, rushes in too late to intercept the pass.
RIGHT: Team Canada's Zarley Zalapski.

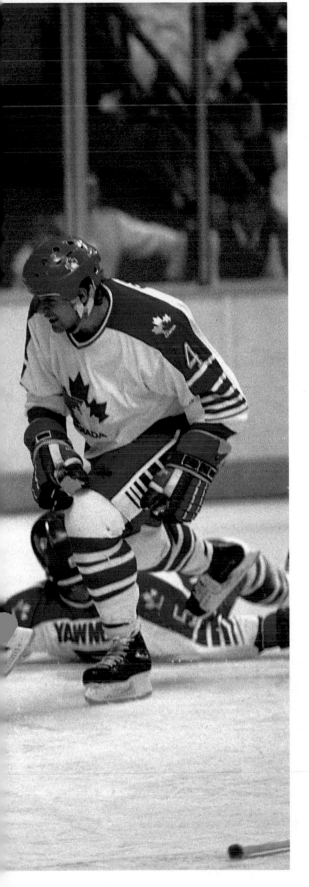

Team Canada had some grounds for optimism: the Soviet Union had not won a world hockey tournament in two years, and last year's Canada Cup and Izvestia tournaments had dimmed their aura of invincibility considerably. But at the Olympic Winter Games the Soviets once again looked unbeatable, whereas Team Canada's four years of preparation were paying off in lackluster play even against mediocre teams. Canada's encounter with the Soviets, its first game of the medal round, came ominously early, putting the team in a do-or-die contest with the squad that it was least likely to beat.

For the first period, Team Canada staved off the Soviet attackers by corralling them into the boards at every opportunity, but that left them little time to organize their own offense. Forty-five seconds into the second period, Moscow winger Serguei Jachine broke the scoreless tie by sneaking a wraparound goal past the post while Sean Burke was looking the other way. It was a demoralizing goal, the kind that makes the players feel the game is not going their way. Team Canada never recovered its stride. About five minutes later, while the Canadians were killing their third unanswered penalty, Viatcheslav Bykov beat Burke at close range. After that, the Soviets skated circles around their opponents and enriched their shutout by three more goals. The loss, combined with Sweden's earlier win over the Czechs, left Canada with no more than a remote mathematical chance at a bronze.

The Saddledome crowd, so vociferous in the first half of the game, was crushed. The next night the arena would fill up for another Olympic spectacle, the far less brutal sport of figure skating. Canadians would watch. They would be amazed and thrilled. But hockey, that armored clash between countries, is unlike other sports. And for the Canadians who feel passionate about it, Team Canada's fall will linger in memory like a lost war.

Nordic Combined

ABOVE:
A spectator arrives at the nordic combined event in Canmore ready to make a lot of noise.

The complex procedures of the nordic combined were no doubt a little puzzling to the untrained North American eye. But the race went something like this. Benefiting from a huge lead in the ski jump portion of the nordic combined team event, the Federal Republic of Germany was given a head start in the cross-country relay portion, and with that advantage the FRG's anchorman was the first across the finish line, although the Swiss had a faster time. The Swiss took silver after slashing their start deficit of four minutes and fifty-two seconds down to just three and a half seconds.

RIGHT:
Pushing hard against the clock, Hubert Schwarz of the FRG helps put his team in first place in the 3-x-10-kilometre team relay portion of the nordic combined event.

Switzerland came close to snatching the gold from the Federal Republic of Germany in the cross-country portion of the nordic combined. Less than four seconds separated their final times.

Figure Skating

The future of compulsory figures had become a point of some contention in the skating world. For some athletes, including Katarina Witt of the German Democratic Republic, tracing school figures—like practicing scales—was an unworthy event for public competition. But U.S. skater Debi Thomas, who excelled at figures, considered them a vital foundation for competition: "The whole reason figure skating is called figure skating," she professed, "is figures." For an essentially boring contest, the compulsory figures event received a lot of attention. But then it represented 30 percent of the skaters' final marks and was a major factor in deciding who would be the 1988 Olympic figure skating queen.

In a long, arduous ordeal that started at eight o'clock in the morning, the competitors attempted to etch perfect circles and loops into the ice. Unsurprisingly, Soviet skater Kira Ivanova placed first, followed by Thomas and Witt. Less predictably, however, the contest put Canada's Elizabeth Manley into an excellent position to vie for a medal. Placing fourth in compulsory figures, Manley was ecstatic. "I truly believe I can beat Kira Ivanova in the free style," she said. "I'm just going to let Debi and Katarina be involved with their own battle."

Ski Jumping

Finland's Matti Nykanen never said he was going after three gold medals; had he failed, people would have been disappointed. But after adding the third and final jewel to his Olympic triple crown for the 90-metre team ski jump, he admitted that it had indeed been his goal. On Day 12 Nykanen once again exceeded his competitors' distances by a comfortable margin with jumps of 114.5 and 115.5 metres. His three teammates also performed capably, putting the Finnish team well in front of their closest rival, Yugoslavia. But Norway stole the bronze from Czechoslovakia after a startling jump by Erik Johnsen. Long hair trailing from his helmet, Johnsen jumped 111.5 metres and helped win Norway's first Olympic ski jump medal in twenty years. Still, as his competitors searched for appropriate accolades, all the talk was about the Flying Finn. Said Canada's Todd Gillman: "He seems to have a feel for the air that no one else has."

RIGHT:
Matti Nykanen is hoisted aloft after he and his teammates won the team ski jumping event. Only following the victory did Nykanen admit he had hoped to win three gold medals at the Olympics.

FAR RIGHT:
Flying to a golden landing, Matti Nykanen once again proves his mettle.

Alpine Skiing

Perennial champion Maria Walliser of Switzerland tears downhill in the giant slalom. Her third-place finish left her behind her teammate, 1987 World Cup champion Vreni Schneider, and Christa Kinshofer-Guethlein of the Federal Republic of Germany.

The Swiss, whose alpine ego was seriously eroded at the Games, reentered the spotlight in the women's giant slalom on the sun-warmed slopes of Mount Allan. Vreni Schneider took the gold, with her more celebrated teammate Maria Walliser settling for bronze. One of the least glamorous members of the Swiss team, Schneider has proven that she is probably one of the circuit's most consistent contenders. And despite the prominence of Walliser and Figini, she said, "I've never felt in the shadow of the rest of the team." Meanwhile, the Federal Republic of Germany's Christa Kinshofer-Guethlein staged a comeback to take the silver medal. Although not considered a major threat, she expected that if she was going to win any medal it would be in slalom rather than giant slalom. "In 1980 I was the favorite for a gold medal in giant slalom and won the silver in slalom," she recalled. "This time I came here to be a winner in slalom and get one in giant slalom. It's crazy, but that's the Olympics."

Short Track Speed Skating

ABOVE:
Ainhoa Ibarra Astelarra of Spain was just one of many who wiped out on the giant slalom slopes. Also down were Karen Percy and Michelle McKendry of Canada.

Great Britain's Wilf O'Reilly once spent his ice time perfecting pirouettes. From age seven to twelve, he studied figure skating—until he saw a short track speed skating championship in his hometown of Birmingham, England, and decided to set his blades on an utterly different course. "In figure skating," says O'Reilly, "the wealthier you are, the better you get. In short track, it doesn't cost a whole heap of money to get yourself in shape. It costs time." Now twenty-three, O'Reilly collected his second gold medal after winning the 1000-metre final with a world record time. Canada's Michel Daignault crossed the line just one stride behind him to take silver. And in the women's 3000-metres, Quebec's Sylvie Daigle placed second after Japan's Eiko Shishii shattered another world record.

DAY 13

Olympians do not dress like ordinary mortals. Lugers are encased in plastic; speed skaters are sheathed like hooded superheroes, and skiers flex and swing with all the flash of toy Transformers. Sleek, vivid, and sexy, Olympic clothes are a crucial part of the Olympic spectacle. But occasionally what an athlete wears can be as influential as how an athlete performs. That fact became all too clear on the thirteenth day of the Games, as the Canadian men's ski team entered the giant slalom in a spanking new set of red and yellow suits that had not been inspected to see if they complied with Olympic standards. After the race, officials discovered that none of the Canadians was wearing a "plomb," the coin-sized seal of approval that was supposed to be affixed to each suit. Consequently, the whole team was disqualified from the giant slalom event, joining ranks with the Bolivians, Moroccans, and Taiwanese, whose skiers also failed to meet the dress code. The Canadians, however, were so far off the pace that disqualification was more embarrassing than damaging. That evening, costumes again became an issue as Katarina Witt and Debi Thomas faced off in figure skating's short program. Witt's outfit, a hip-baring blue number decked with rhinestones and ostrich plumes, was already infamous. Canadian coach Peter Dunfield had been quoted as saying a skater should wear "a dress and not a G-string." Even visiting sex therapist Dr. Ruth Westheimer got into the act, suggesting the Eastern Bloc ice princess should show "a little decorum so as not to arouse the judges." But the judges didn't seem to mind. Thomas, who wore a black spangled leotard, enthralled the audience and scored the highest technical marks. Yet Witt outflanked her American rival with higher points for presentation—prompting an outburst of criticism from Thomas' coach. Apparently, a fight for gold could come down to a contest of styles.

In glitter and plumes, Katarina Witt, reigning queen, defends her crown with coquettish charm.

Figure Skating

Clearly pleased with her own flawless and brash performance, Debi Thomas waves to the cheering crowd.

On the one hand, it was a display of pure form: the crisp sound of blades shearing ice and the sight of bodies twirling through double axels, triple jumps, layback spins, flying camels . . . On the other hand, the women's short program presented a farfetched exchange of cultural stereotypes. A Yugoslav skated to the theme from *Dr. Zhivago*; a Belgian opted for American bluegrass, and an Italian, in a cruel stroke of irony, punctuated "There's No Business Like Show Business" with two bad falls. Meanwhile, Katarina Witt, the GDR star from Karl Marx Stadt, put a new spin on dialectical materialism by skating to a medley of Broadway show

"I wanted to have fun," Elizabeth Manley of Canada said after her exuberant performance.

tunes including "Hello, Dolly." Amid all the razzmatazz, it was refreshing to see ponytailed Midori Ito from Japan galvanize the crowd with a brilliant performance set to traditional Japanese music. Though not among the top-seeded group of skaters, Ito took fourth place in the short program. And Canada's Elizabeth Manley, handling a difficult program with aplomb, fulfilled her goal of placing third.

Although the evening counted for only 20 percent of the marks that would decide the medal, it provided the first clear glimpse of how the judges viewed the skaters' talents. The main contestants could not have been more dissimilar: Witt, the flirtatious, fair-skinned queen of the ball, versus Thomas, the athletic, exuberant black American challenger. Squeezing her coach's hand until the last moment, Witt went out to charm and seduce with the teasing moves of a cabaret vamp. As for Thomas, she gave her coach a high five then tore up the ice to the sound of beat-box funk that could have come from a ghetto blaster in Harlem. Both acts were flawless, although Thomas—despite her lower style marks—displayed more energy, ambition, and no nonsense emotion. Later, in an unusual breach of protocol, her coach, Alex McGowan, seemed to cast a shadow over her fate. "I am a little concerned," he said, "that no matter what Debi does, the die is cast."

Alpine Skiing

For Alberto Tomba, the Bologna Bullet, there was more at stake than a gold medal as he powered his way down the giant slalom course at Nakiska. The skier's father, a textile merchant, had sweetened the pot with the promise of a red Ferrari. The winner of seven World Cup races during the winter, Tomba let his fans down earlier in the week by falling at the top of the super giant slalom. But by Thursday he was back to form, as he knifed his way down the giant slalom course with unrivaled tenacity and speed. Bashing through the gates, the powerful Italian finished the two heats with a combined time that was more than a second faster than his closest competitor, Austria's Hubert Strolz. The immodest Tomba, an Italian playboy who once called himself "the new messiah of skiing," said: "The gold medal is nice. It gives me a certain prestige when I meet other great stars like Katarina Witt." Meanwhile, Swiss choirboy Pirmin Zurbriggen again had to scale down his Olympic ambitions, taking only the bronze.

Tiger Shaw of the USA cuts it close on a gate in the giant slalom. He finished twelfth and was the highest-ranking American.

The Nakiska event was overshadowed by a tragedy on the slopes. Jorg Oberhammer, a doctor with the Austrian Ski Federation, was killed instantly when he slid under the tracks of a snow-grooming machine after colliding with another skier. Zurbriggen and team-mate Martin Hangl witnessed the accident from a chair lift. Hangl was so shaken that he withdrew from the race. Though Zurbriggen decided not to drop out, he said he could not stop thinking about it as he left the starting gate.

Supported by second-place Hubert Strolz and third-place Pirmin Zurbriggen, Alberto Tomba of Italy kicks up his heels in triumph.

Cross-Country Skiing

No sport in the Winter Games was more dominated by a single country than cross-country skiing. And in the final women's event, the 20-kilometre race, the Soviet machine swept all three medals, with Tamara Tikhonova taking the gold. The victory brought the Soviets' cross-country medal total to thirteen. However, on the same day that the Canadian alpine team was disqualified for wearing unapproved ski suits, a Soviet competitor in the cross-country event, Nina Gavriliouk, became the first Olympic athlete to be penalized for commercialism: she wore a headband with an Adidas logo on it. Canada's top-ranked contender, Angela Schmidt Foster—whose Olympic ordeal ended as dismally as it began—placed forty-fourth. "It wasn't even close to what I can do," she said. "I'm relieved it's over. I've kind of had enough."

RIGHT:
Silver medal winner Anfissa Reztsova of the USSR finished the 20-kilometre cross-country race nineteen seconds behind teammate Tamara Tikhonova.

FAR RIGHT:
Marie Andree Masson of Canada was disappointed with her performance. She started well in the 20-kilometre race but slipped behind and finished twenty-seventh.

Hockey

For Canadians, hockey was a subject better left undiscussed in the aftermath of Team Canada's 5-0 loss to the Soviets on Wednesday. But Americans, who had placed so much faith in their team, had suffered a similar disappointment much earlier in the tournament when their hopes were snuffed out by the Federal Republic of Germany. For the United States, the denouement took place on Thursday, as its team defeated Switzerland 8-4 to claim seventh place in the twelve-team tournament. Asked if he thought his players performed up to their potential, coach Dave Peterson said, "The team played very well. They acquitted themselves well, and they have nothing to apologize for."

Short Track Speed Skating

Traditionally, European and North American athletes have held a monopoly on medals in the Winter Games. But in the demonstration sport of short track speed skating, Far East nations found an opportunity to assert themselves. Following up Korea's Ki Hoon Kim's gold medal victory in the 1500-metres at short skating's Olympic debut on Monday, Korean Joon Ho Lee won gold in Thursday's 3000-metre event. And in the women's 1000-metre final, Yan Li of the People's Republic of China struck gold—the first medal of any kind ever won by a Chinese athlete at a Winter Olympics. After the final day of short track demonstration events, Canada had won ten medals—twice as many as any other nation competing. But Canadian skater Sylvie Daigle mounted the podium with reluctance to accept her final medal, a silver for the 1000-metres, which she felt rightly belonged to her teammate Maryse Perreault. Rounding the last bend in the event's final race, Perreault had been heading for second place when a skater coming up from behind hit her and sent her sprawling to the ice.

In short track speed skating, falls are common, especially on the corners, where the ice is slicked down. Although skaters wear helmets, knee pads, and shin guards, injuries do occur.

Freestyle Skiing

ABOVE:
Hermann Reitberger of the Federal Republic of Germany won the men's ballet freestyle skiing. Freestyle skiing was popular with the public and attracted the largest crowds of any nonofficial Olympic event.

RIGHT:
Christine Rossi of France demonstrates a new kind of pole vault. She took the gold in the women's ballet freestyle skiing, a demonstration event at the Olympics.

Over the past decade, freestyle skiing has come a long way from the days of hotdoggers who showed off for their friends by doing flips off cornices. And there could be no better evidence of the sport's search for sophistication than the freestyle ballet event at Olympic Park in which skiers incorporated tricks from figure skating, gymnastics, and dance.

Canadian Dave Walker's bid for a medal was dashed after he injured his shoulder midway through a difficult twist. Hermann Reitberger of the Federal Republic of Germany, a ten-year World Cup veteran, won the men's ballet event. Christine Rossi of France took gold in the women's event. Despite the freestyle's demonstration status, Rossi said, "In France, they will look at this event the same way they look at all the other sports in the Olympics."

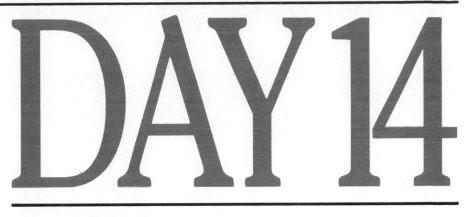

DAY 14

By leading in the medals race, two Eastern Bloc countries — the Soviet Union and the German Democratic Republic — had shown they had a patented formula for minting Olympic gold: discipline. And there was no disciplinarian more notorious than Viktor Tikhonov, the steely-eyed Red Army colonel behind the bench of the Soviet hockey team. Earlier, some had said that Tikhonov's time was up. His spartan style was unfashionably dour in the new age of glasnost, his team had suffered a string of embarrassing defeats, and he had been criticized by both the Soviet press and one of his own players. But as Tikhonov's red machine rolled over all contenders to clinch gold two days before the end of the tournament, it became clear that his hockey dynasty was far from finished. The Soviets celebrated their 7-1 obliteration of Sweden with uncharacteristic abandon, carrying on like an NHL team that had won the Stanley Cup. They hugged, they kissed, and one player tossed up his stick as an offering to the crowd. Even Tikhonov jumped for joy and reached up to shake the outstretched hands of spectators. The same day at the Olympic Oval, another coach watched as his charges transcended expectations. Ernst Luding of the German Democratic Republic was delighted to see his star, Karin Kania, streak to a world record finish in the 1000-metre speed skating event. He assumed that her time would serve as a secure down payment on a gold, since she had beaten her only serious rival in the event, American Bonnie Blair. But just minutes later another woman wearing GDR double-blue, Christa Rothenburger, came out of nowhere to render her teammate's record obsolete. Luding — Rothenburger's fiancé as well as her coach — was overjoyed. Enthusiastically rushing over to give her a hug, he slipped and fell in a heap at her feet. Discipline had finally given way to delirium.

Discipline pays off in gold as the Soviets win the hockey tournament.

Hockey

The hit men of international hockey dispatched Sweden with machine-gun efficiency. A volley of three goals within a span of one minute and forty-one seconds in the first period did the trick. After that, the Soviets simply relaxed into their familiar groove of synchronized passing and freestyle skating, while the Swedes chased the puck like prisoners in a pinball game—just as Team Canada did two days earlier. What helped clinch the gold medal for the Soviets so prematurely, however, was Czechoslovakia's 5-2 upset over Finland. The Czechs, who were already eliminated from medal contention, became the spoilers by ruining Finland's five-game undefeated streak in a scrappy, ill-tempered contest. Stepping out of character, the Czechs played an unusually physical style of hockey. And hitting four goalposts and a crossbar, they had scoring opportunities to spare. Meanwhile, Team Canada followed its demoralizing loss to the Soviets with a little catharsis—an 8-1 victory over the Federal Republic of Germany that kept them within mathematical reach of a bronze.

BELOW:
Andy Moog, Team Canada's goalie, watches the puck go by. Moog let in only one goal, and Canada beat the Federal Republic of Germany 8-1.

FAR RIGHT:
Finnish goalie Jarmo Myllys faced twenty-six shots on goal in a bitter game against Czechoslovakia.

Biathlon

No one expected Canada to win a medal in the 4-x-7.5-kilometre biathlon relay, since the sport is still relatively fresh in North America. But no one expected Canada to fare as poorly as it did. Out of a field of fifteen countries, only Korea finished behind the Canadian team. Inaccurate shooting was the main reason for the team's failure. Quebec's Charles Plamondon, the nation's highest-ranked biathlete going into the Olympics, got into trouble early on when he had to ski three penalty loops after missing targets. The Soviet Union maintained its tight grip on Canmore medals by winning the gold. The Federal Republic of Germany took silver, and the bronze went to Italy.

Speed Skating

Many in the crowd at the Olympic Oval had brought the Stars and Stripes and come to cheer on Bonnie Blair. Then Karin Kania of the German Democratic Republic, skating in long and powerful strides, bettered Blair's time by more than half a second and broke her own world record at the 1000-metre event. The crowd fell so silent that the announcer asked for some noise to celebrate the feat. When the gun sounded for the final pair of racers, Kania was still cruising the ice, winding down from her world record skate, and the crowd seemed to have lost interest. Covering the ice in the short, chopping steps of a sprinter, Kania's teammate Christa Rothenburger pushed herself to the limit—and shaved one-fiftieth of a second off Kania's new record. It was the first time that Rothenburger had beaten her teammate in the 1000-metres.

The victory put Rothenburger in a unique position. A former sprint cycling champion, she also had her eye on the 1988 Summer Olympics in Seoul. Only one Olympian has ever won golds in both Summer and Winter Games—American Eddie Eagen, light heavyweight boxing champion at Antwerp in 1920 and a member of the winning four-man bob team at Lake Placid in 1932. "I have only completed one of my wishes," said Rothenburger after her victory. "The second one, I'll find out about in September or October."

Throughout the Games, records fell at the new Olympic Oval. All previous Olympic speed skating races had been held outdoors.

Alpine Skiing

ABOVE:
Switzerland's remarkable Vreni Schneider checks out the course carefully before the slalom, in which she took the gold medal.

Before the Olympic Games, Vreni Schneider's name didn't come up too often in all the media's stories about star athletes who were expected to win. Everyone was too obsessed with her Swiss teammates, Maria Walliser and Michela Figini: their rivalry made a good yarn, and Walliser (along with Katarina Witt) aspired to be a movie star. But Schneider, after winning Wednesday's giant slalom, quietly skied to her second gold medal victory of the Games with a seamless showing in the slalom. Afterward she promised that victory would not spoil her. "Everybody wants to make a star out of me," she said, "but I don't want to be a star. I just want to race, and to race well." Meanwhile, Yugoslav Mateja Svet upset higher-ranked competitors to take the silver, the first Olympic medal ever won by Yugoslavia in a women's alpine event. Svet had high praise for Schneider, saying, "She could be the Alberto Tomba of the women's circuit." With a laugh, Schneider retorted: "Oh no, don't compare me to him."

RIGHT:
Michelle McKendry attacks the slalom course. Finishing eighteenth, she was one of only two Canadians to complete the race.

DAY 15

The script was written. The stage was set. And according to all the advance billing, the drama would climax in a showdown between two skaters, each interpreting the same operatic tragedy, a clash of Carmens. Like the Orser-Boitano contest exactly one week earlier, the duel between Katarina Witt and Debi Thomas had taken on the dimensions of an Olympian prizefight, with no room in the ring for lesser gods. But in mid-act fate rewrote the script in a way that neither the actors nor the audience could have foreseen. Canada's Elizabeth Manley, who had modestly said she would be grateful for bronze, blew onto the ice in a hot pink dress with the force of the last Olympic chinook. Defying skeptics who had warned that even the bronze might slip through her nervous fingers, she stole the spotlight away from the stars and never let go of it. As the judges awarded her the highest marks of the evening and bouquets littered the ice, the Saddledome thundered with a standing ovation. Backstage, Debi Thomas could hear the clamor. She was the last to skate. She had waited a long time for her moment, perhaps too long. She didn't feel right as she took to the ice, and her fears were horribly confirmed as she faltered on the landing of her first combination jump. Instantly, the fight went out of her. Stumbling a second and third time, her Olympic dream became a nightmare as Carmen's tragedy was eclipsed by her own. A shell-shocked audience tried to absorb what had happened. Then, realizing that Thomas had lost not only to Witt but to Manley, tragedy turned to triumph, and they were on their feet, cheering wildly for an outcome they had never dreamed possible. Orser's silver came as a letdown; Manley's was as good as gold, a magical finale to the Games. For the host country, it arrived like a surprise party at the end of a long day. The Canadians at Calgary had tried to do everything right, but so often others had taken the glory. Now they had a miracle they could call their own.

Wearing a white Stetson given her by a fan, Elizabeth Manley, in disbelief, takes in the audience's rapturous response to her performance.

Figure Skating

Katarina Witt skated with confidence and style to take the gold, making her the first woman since 1936 to win figure skating gold medals in two successive Olympics.

The first indication that the universe was not unfolding along predictable lines came when Japan's Midori Ito drew the sort of tumultuous ovation normally reserved for hometown favorites. With her acrobatics and her smile, Ito had stolen the crowd's heart in the short program two days earlier, and Calgary had not forgotten her. In a costume that shimmered fish-scale blue, she electrified her fans from the first jump. Racing backward toward the boards at perilous speed, Ito leapt into a difficult triple lutz at the last moment—the first of *seven* triple jumps in a breath-taking program. Winning the highest technical marks of the evening, she wept with joy. But her low score in compulsory figures, combined with ungenerous marks for artistic impression, deprived her of a medal.

By contrast, the response to Katarina Witt's appearance was eerily subdued. Wearing a fiery red dress with flamenco ruffles, the 1984 gold medalist skated a cautious program that put the accent on artistry. As her skate blades carved the ice, scarlet fingernails traced the air. This was Witt the aspiring actress as much as Witt the skater, Witt the Carmenologist who had immersed herself in the character of the murdered heroine by reading books,

"I'm sorry," Debi Thomas whispered to coach Alex McGowan after her disappointing final performance.

attending the opera, and studying film and video versions of the story. To no one's surprise, her interpretation won high points for artistic impression, but her lower technical marks left Thomas ample room to overtake her.

On the morning of the competition, while other skaters were practicing, Elizabeth Manley was doing her laundry at the Calgary Olympic Village. All the focus directed toward Witt and Thomas, she said, helped her relax. Here was a Canadian with a passion not for *Carmen* but for television soap operas, a skater who was deeply superstitious and never traveled without a teddy bear. Manley's volatile nerves had marred her performance at the 1987 world championships, and there were doubts she could remain calm in the storm of Olympic competition. But a week before the Games opened, Manley crossed a new threshold of confidence after waking up from a dream in a sweat. She dreamed that she skated a perfect performance in the Saddledome, although she lost her focus after landing the difficult triple lutz. In the final free skate, Manley saw her dream come true, even to the point of losing focus after the triple lutz, then recovering it in time to land a triple toe-loop moments later. Overjoyed even before seeing her marks, the Canadian in the hot pink dress accepted a Stetson tossed from the stands, and crowned herself queen. "That crowd was completely overwhelming," she recalled. "I could have stayed out all night."

Manley won the free skate and seemed destined for bronze in overall competition. Then, with the soap opera twist of Thomas' faltering ordeal, she was suddenly elevated from a supporting to a starring role. Canada had found the silver lining to its Olympic dream.

Shimmering in the light, Midori Ito spins in the air.

Bobsleigh

Despite mild temperatures, the ice on Olympic Park's refrigerated track withstood the punishment of the four-man bobsleigh event. At the end of round one, Wolfgang Hoppe, who won double gold at Sarajevo in 1984, was in first place. The Soviet Union's Ianis Kipours, seeking an encore of his gold medal victory in Monday's two-man event, placed second. And Canadian driver Chris Lori steered his red and white sled to ninth place. Lori raced in Calgary even though he had broken his collarbone twice in 1987. "It was all so frustrating," he said of the past year. "Sometimes I feel like someone keeps kicking me in the butt and won't stop."

RIGHT:
An Italian bobsleigh team leaps aboard.

FOLLOWING PAGES:
Looking like science fiction creatures, the four-man bobsleigh team of GDR-II gathers speed.

Speed Skating

ABOVE:
Gold medal winner Yvonne van Gennip of the Netherlands is congratulated by Gunda Kleemann of the GDR.

For the second time in a week, the Netherlands' Yvonne van Gennip struck gold by outracing the German Democratic Republic's formidable speed skating team. Karin Kania and Andrea Ehrig of the GDR settled for silver and bronze, respectively, as van Gennip zoomed to a new Olympic record in the 1500-metre event. For Kania—the world's top-ranked female speed skater during the past four years—the race culminated a frustrating week in which her efforts were hampered by a cold. "We can't be best all the time," Kania remarked. "The time will come when people are happy about medals and not only gold medals."

RIGHT:
Natalie Grenier of Canada relaxes after a grueling race. She placed eleventh in the 1500-metre speed skating event.

Alpine Skiing

Living up to his own bombast, Alberto "La Bomba" Tomba stole thunder—and lightning—from Pirmin Zurbriggen by winning the men's slalom in spectacular style. After receiving his second gold medal of the Games, Tomba followed through on the boast he had made after winning the giant slalom two days earlier: his intention to meet "other great stars like Katarina Witt." Tomba went straight from the medal ceremony to the Saddledome. Other athletes, including Moscow's Ekaterina Gordeeva and Edmonton's Wayne Gretzky, came to watch the figure skating. But Tomba arrived, rose in hand, to introduce himself to a star. Later Witt said, "It was fun meeting him because he doesn't know much about figure skating and I don't know much about his sport." She laughed and added, "I couldn't understand him because he spoke Italian."

Pirmin Zurbriggen had hoped to sweep the alpine events, but his dreams failed to materialize as race after race slipped away. He finished seventh in the slalom.

By winning the slalom, Alberto "La Bomba" Tomba proved again that his boasts weren't all bombast. This was his second gold of the Games.

Italian fans show the colors in support of Tomba.

Cross-Country Skiing

By the time Mexico's Roberto Adolfo Alvarez Hojel staggered across the finish line of the 50-kilometre cross-country marathon, the winners had already received their medals. In fact, Alvarez had reached only the halfway mark when gold medal winner Gunde Svan of Sweden secured his victory. At one point officials sent two skiers into the woods to make sure Alvarez was all right. But the Mexican persevered. When he emerged from a blizzard three and a half hours after he had started the race, there was hardly anyone on hand to watch him become the last of sixty-one skiers to finish. His mother presented him with a blanket and a box of Oreo cookies. "I'm exhausted," said Alvarez. "I'm going to have a beer."

Hockey

A high five in a well-played game in which Team Canada restored some of its wounded pride by beating Czechoslovakia 6-3.

Team Canada retrieved some of its lost pride with a spirited final game, defeating Czechoslovakia 6-3. Andy Moog played an exceptional game in goal, thwarting Czech forward Igor Liba twice—first on breakaway, then with a lunging dive across the crease to stop a goal that Liba had already begun to celebrate. The victory allowed Canada to cling to its hopes for a bronze by a slim mathematical thread. From now on the only game left for the Canadians to play was armchair odds-making.

DAY 16

It was clear and windless, a good day for bobsledding. Early in the morning, as if the Games could not end without a last kick of unscheduled drama, the Jamaican bobsleigh team lost control rounding a curve at 120 kilometres per hour and rolled their sled, scraping their helmets against the chute. All four walked away with no more than bruises, then started shaking hands with spectators, Eddy-Edwards-style. It was a close call, but as with the Games themselves — so often thrown off course by the unofficial whims of the weather — the worst was averted. Despite setbacks, the Games ended a success, with all the events completed by the closing day. And those who came to watch and compete were left with fond memories of the warmth of Calgary's climate and people. That evening at the Closing Ceremony, there was barely a breeze to ripple the Olympic flag as it was lowered at McMahon Stadium. And it was not too cold for the short-skirted skaters who danced on the world's largest temporary ice rink. In the stands, 60 000 people holding red-shaded candles sent an illuminated "wave" circling round the stadium again and again like a vast sea anemone undulating through the night with thousands of glowing tendrils. The wave eventually stopped long enough for IOC president Juan Antonio Samaranch to declare the Games closed. A groan escaped from the crowd. And as the Olympic flame subsided, slipping below the cauldron's rim like a setting sun, hundreds of flashbulbs winked back from the crowd in an attempt to catch it. There was a tangible sadness. Two skaters danced to delicate music. Then the mood lifted with tributes to the next generation of Olympians. Fireworks filled the sky; cancan cowgirls skated a mock shoot-out, and athletes broke rank and swarmed the stage to dance a hoedown. It was Calgary's farewell to the five-ringed magic: the world's biggest road show was moving on.

An Austrian four-man bobsleigh team speeds down the track.

Bobsleigh

The four-man bobsleigh team of the GDR's Wolfgang Hoppe was favored for a gold, but came in second behind the Swiss team headed by Ekkehard Fasser.

There were two upsets in the final day of the four-man bobsleigh. One involved the Jamaican sled, which flipped over at high speed and sent its occupants on a bruising ride down the ice-covered chute. The other involved the Swiss sled, which sped down the track right side up to snatch a gold medal from the German Democratic Republic. Wolfgang Hoppe's GDR team, leading after Saturday's heats, was strongly favored to win the event. But Ekkehard Fasser, a thirty-five-year-old veteran of the sport, piloted the Swiss to victory, breaking the track record in one of the heats. And as his green and blue sled thundered down the track, it sounded not unlike a runaway train, with the clanging of cowbells by Swiss fans adding to the effect.

Nordic Combined

It was a busy day for the Renaissance men of nordic combined. Because of previous delays, the ski jump and cross-country events had to be crammed into the same day—the first time in Olympic history that that had occurred. After competing in the 70-metre ski jump, Switzerland's Hippolyt Kempf listened to some quiet jazz on his Walkman as he commuted from Calgary's Olympic Park to the cross-country course at Canmore. After a third-place finish in the jumping, he did not expect to win gold. Starting the cross-country race thirty-one seconds behind Austria's Klaus Sulzenbacher (who earned a head start by placing first in the ski jump), Kempf eventually caught up with Sulzenbacher, then pulled into the lead. "He was so fast and so strong," said Sulzenbacher, "and I was so tired that I couldn't hold him."

Speed Skating

ABOVE:
Yvonne van Gennip of the Netherlands strides to her third gold medal of the Olympic Games. She and Matti Nykanen were the only athletes to get a hat trick in gold.

Dutch speed skater Yvonne van Gennip was not considered a top contender when she arrived in Calgary, since she had undergone surgery on her right foot only two months earlier. "I had no idea when I came here that I would win a gold medal," she said. "A bronze would have been nice." But in the final day's 5000-metre event, van Gennip defeated the German Democratic Republic's speed skating powerhouse for the third time in the Games—and became the second athlete at the Games to win three gold medals. This upset marked the end of an era for the GDR team. Veterans Karin Kania, Andrea Ehrig, and Christa Rothenburger were all expected to retire after the Games.

RIGHT:
Elena Belci of Italy glides to a halt after finishing twelfth in the 5000-metre speed skating event.

Hockey

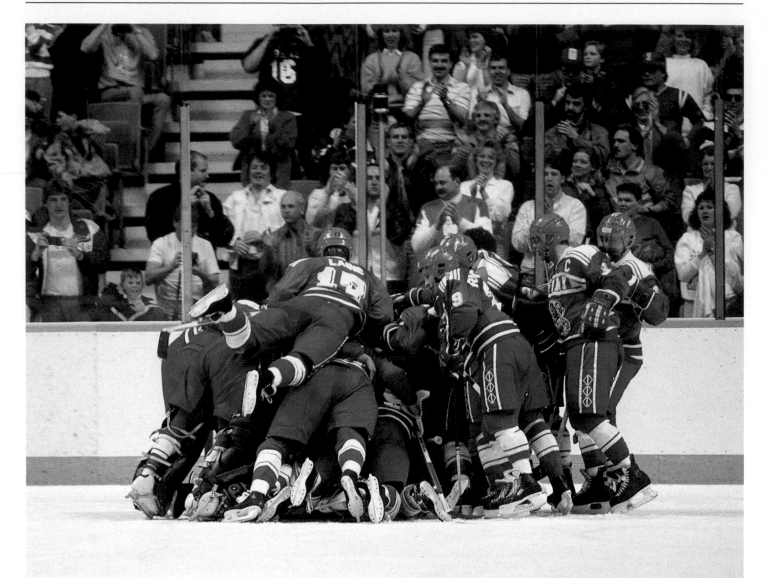

The victorious Finnish hockey team piles up. They were the only team to beat the Soviets.

On the final day of the Games, Team Canada's players became fans, rooting for a home team called the Federal Republic of Germany. An FRG win against the Swedes would have meant a bronze medal for Canada. And goalie Karl Friesen was especially motivated to help the Canadian cause: he was born in Winnipeg. However, although he blocked thirty-nine shots in an exceptional display of goaltending, Friesen could not prevent the Swedes from edging his team 3-2. Sweden then saw its silver promise take on a bronze tarnish as Finland added an ironic conclusion to a tournament that had taken some bizarre turns. The Finns, who suffered an embarrassing defeat to Switzerland in their opening game, erased the shame and stole the silver with a 2-1 upset over the Soviet Union. It was the Soviets' only loss in a tournament where—without the challenge from the NHL's top professionals—they regained international supremacy. Olympic gold served as the incentive; once they had captured it, the motivation was gone.

Figure Skating

For once, it was just an exhibition. After all the strain and tension of Olympic competition, the world's finest figure skaters performed for the sheer love of it. The Saddledome was darkened; the scoreboard was blank; spotlights swept the ice. The star couples of the Soviet Union—Gordeeva and Grinkov, Valova and Vassiliev, Boukine and Bestemianova—each took one last turn around the dance floor. Orser and Boitano, no longer locked in an Olympian duel, showed that the essence of their art was more lyrical than martial. And Orser, as if to explain himself, opened his heart to the audience, then showed he could still fly like no one else. Manley relived her triumph in the same pink dress she wore the night before; Witt sparkled as a silver diva. And then, showing that there was some punk in the princess, Witt donned a rhinestone-studded leather jacket and danced to Michael Jackson's "Bad." But perhaps the bravest was Debi Thomas. Less than twenty-four hours after her harrowing defeat, she was back—dressed defiantly in gold—and skating the blues.

ABOVE:
Brian Orser thrills the audience at the Saddledome.

RIGHT:
Debi Thomas returns to the spotlight at the figure skating exhibition.

Closing Ceremony

In the end, Calgary's sixteen-day extravaganza was hailed as the most successful Winter Games in Olympic history. And like so much of what transpired during the Games, the event that ended them was unprecedented: it was the first time that a Winter Games closing ceremony had been held outdoors. Under the spell of benevolent weather, it was a more relaxed affair than the Opening Ceremony. There was more than a trace of nostalgia as figure skating champions from past Olympics made cameo appearances

Lighting up the night: fireworks and thousands of candles at the Closing Ceremony.

on a floodlit rink while a larger cast skated a pageant of pioneer history. The crowd felt an inevitable sense of loss when the flame was extinguished. But as the music picked up and the dancing resumed, the athletes—finally released from the pressures of competition—were in a mood to celebrate. Soon they would return to far-flung corners of the earth, some already looking forward to another chance at Olympic glory, others simply cherishing the memories. At the Calgary Games, a temporary oasis of harmony amid international discord, the youth of the world gave fresh meaning to the Olympic ideal. And soon the Olympic spirit—that secular flame next to leap continents and seasons to Seoul—would burn again.

RIGHT:
The Canadian team waves good-bye to the crowd.

BELOW RIGHT:
The flame that had been lit sixteen days earlier by Robyn Perry was extinguished at the Closing Ceremony.

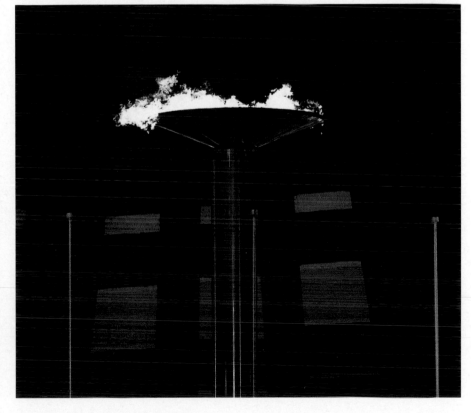

OLYMPIC CELEBRATIONS

PRECEDING PAGES:
Olympic Plaza during nightly celebration.

ABOVE:
Athletes of USSR, Switzerland, and Sweden at the Opening Ceremony.

LEFT:
The RCMP's famed Musical Ride at the Opening Ceremony.

RIGHT:
Canadian athletes wave to the crowd.

LEFT:
Native dancers performed at Olympic Plaza.

ABOVE:
Shaw Festival's *You Never Can Tell* was a hit at the Arts Festival.

FAR RIGHT:
A shaman's rattle from *The Spirit Sings* exhibition at the Glenbow Museum.

Pin-trading mania swept the streets of Calgary during the Games.

LEFT:
A dancer at Olympic Plaza, where crowds gathered nightly.

ABOVE:
The Calgary Opera's performance of *Porgy and Bess* was well received by Arts Festival audiences.

RIGHT:
The Desrosiers Dance Theatre's performance of *Incognito*.

Hot-air balloons—unexpected wonders across the sky.

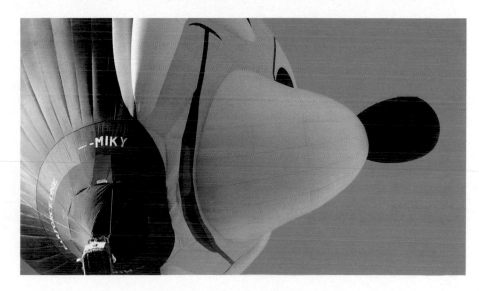

Like the athletes, fans wore colors, hats, and costumes that announced their affiliation—the USA and USSR (left and right).

BELOW:
Italian teammates cheer on the flamboyant Alberto Tomba.

The rodeo—a longtime Calgary tradition—came to town for the Olympics.

TOP:
K.D. Lang, a popular and exciting performer, at the Olympic Eve Gala.

ABOVE:
From *The Spirit Sings*, an amulet cluster dating from the mid-1800s.

RIGHT:
The festive Closing Ceremony—end of the celebrations.

Volunteers—thousands strong—helped make the Calgary Games a success and left visitors with warm memories of western hospitality.

TEAM '88

OCO'88 PURPOSE

Calgary was selected as the location of the XV Olympic Winter Games by the International Olympic Committee at Baden-Baden, Federal Republic of Germany, in September 1981.

The Olympic Charter, the document that sets out the main requirements for the organization of the Olympic Games, requires that an Olympic Organizing Committee be established. Accordingly, the XV Olympic Winter Games Organizing Committee (OCO'88) was incorporated in April 1982 for the purpose of planning and staging the Games.

In February 1983, the City of Calgary delegated its responsibilities under the Olympic Charter to OCO'88. Then, in September 1983, the Canadian Olympic Association (COA) entrusted its responsibilities to organize the Games to OCO'88.

Through its early years, the organizing committee maintained a small contingent of full-time staff members and its corporate structure remained in a relatively stable pyramid shape. From 32 employees and approximately 200 volunteers at the end of 1983,

the organizing committee swelled to 92 employees and more than 400 volunteers in December 1985. A year later, staff members had trebled to 270 and active volunteers quadrupled to more than 1600.

Major growth, however, took place in the year preceding the Games. During the final pre-Games countdown, as OCO'88 completed its transition from planning to operations, departments were added and groups created. In addition to chairman Frank King and president Bill Pratt, OCO'88 entered the Games with a twenty-nine-member board of directors, seven groups headed by vice-presidents, fourteen divisions headed by general managers, and thirty-eight departments headed by managers. In addition, more than 75 committees and almost 200 subcommittees formed the volunteer infrastructure.

The final contingent of 490 staff members and 9400 volunteers, collectively known as Team '88, provided an enthusiastic and dedicated work force larger than that of the entire City of Calgary. More than anything else, it was this work force—the members of Team '88—who made the XV Olympic Winter Games come together so successfully.

VOLUNTEERS ARE A CALGARY TRADITION

Volunteers were the lifeblood of the XV Olympic Winter Games Organizing Committee (OCO'88). Without the dedication of thousands of these men and women, the Games quite simply would not have happened.

The organizing committee began recruiting volunteers early. Application forms were widely distributed, and by March 1987, more than 20 000 people had applied. As the forms arrived at OCO'88 offices, the names were entered into a central computer registry, and eventually a volunteer work force of 9400 was established.

In addition to assembling this organization—which, together with almost 500 full-time staff members of OCO'88, came to be known as Team '88 the organizing committee's volunteer division developed programs to train and educate volunteers in the aims of the Olympic movement and of OCO'88, and established ways to provide all volunteers with assessment and recognition.

The organization then set about forming committees. Volunteers' interests, skills, and experience were identified, then matched with the needed services—everything from sports and the torch relay to food services and protocol. In the end, there were more than seventy-five committees involved in staging the Games.

Each committee was structured like a corporation, with a chairman responsible for liaison with the organizing committee. Volunteers filled some of the Games' most important roles—from sport chairmen in charge of the field of play to venue chairmen who controlled all aspects of operations at Olympic venues, from volunteer workers who monitored access at gates to others who kept the sites litter-free.

To provide a central workplace for all these volunteers, OCO'88 constructed the Olympic Volunteer Centre at McMahon Stadium, near the University of Calgary campus. Opened in 1985, the volunteer centre quickly became the hub of volunteer operations. Large-scale meetings and major orientation and training programs were held on the upper floor, which eventually became the location for OCO'88's monthly board of directors meetings. The lower floor, divided into smaller meeting rooms named after locations of previous Winter Games (the Lake Placid Room, the Innsbruck Room) and partitioned off into individual work areas, became the nexus of volunteer involvement. The OVC, as it came to be known within the acronym-laden organizing committee, was one of the organization's masterstrokes before the Games.

Right from the beginning, training the army of volunteer personnel was regarded as one of the organizing committee's most important tasks. In addition to instruction in Olympic sports, Olympic history, and the Olympic movement, volunteers were given training and orientation to prepare them for their roles during the Games.

The volunteer division was also responsible for outfitting the thousands of men and women in Team '88. Within three basic types of clothing (skiwear, casual wear, and business attire), more than fifty unique clothing packages were created, using colors developed to give the Games a unified look throughout the city and at all Olympic venues, sites, and locations. Volunteers working at Stampede Park, for example, were given alpine-blue uniforms, with glacier-gray sleeves indicating sport volunteers and fireweed-magenta sleeves indicating support volunteers. In the clothing program, no distinction was made between staff and volunteers. In this way, Team '88 members presented a consistently smart "dignified western" appearance to the thousands of spectators and millions more who witnessed the events on television.

In all, about 98 000 pieces of clothing, from tuques and gloves to ski jackets and cowboy hats, were manufactured for the Games. For most members of Team '88, the clothing packages became a symbol of prestige, a colorful reminder of their participation in the most exciting winter sports spectacle ever staged in Canada.

The volunteer assessment and recognition committee developed their programs in two stages: one to take place prior to the Games, and the other at their conclusion. Since OCO'88 felt it was important to make people feel part of the team, they frequently asked for feedback from individual volunteers and staff. Each member of Team '88 was also given a gold pin as he or she became active with the organizing committee, and everyone was invited to monthly get-togethers and occasional information forums.

Formal pre-Games recognition was accomplished with an annual dinner and dance. In 1985, the organizing committee played host to 800 volunteers. The following year, more than 2000 people attended Volunteer Recognition Night. In May 1987, eight months before the Games, more than 7000 members of Team '88 attended "the largest party ever held in Calgary."

Post-Games, each Team '88 member was presented with a significant item representing the Olympic Winter Games. A commemorative medal and a certificate were designed and presented to each volunteer and staff member. The organizing committee broke its record of the previous year by saying a good-bye and thank-you to over 10 000 people.

Preview 88, the series of international sport competitions held in 1986 and 1987 to test the newly constructed facilities, also allowed the organizing committee to test its systems. Access control points, accreditation procedures, hosting duties, language interpretation, and a myriad of volunteer functions were tested and refined during these competitions. By the fall of 1987, when the last three Preview 88 competitions were held in short track speed skating, figure skating, and speed skating, Team '88 was a smoothly functioning organization.

The planning that went into Preview 88 paid off during the Games. The outstanding efforts of 9400 volunteers and 490 staff members made the XV Olympic Winter Games come together.

RESULTS OF THE GAMES

MEDAL STANDINGS OF THE XV OLYMPIC WINTER GAMES

	gold	silver	bronze	total
Soviet Union	11	9	9	29
German Democratic Republic	9	10	6	25
Switzerland	5	5	5	15
Austria	3	5	2	10
Federal Republic of Germany	2	4	2	8
Finland	4	1	2	7
Netherlands	3	2	2	7
Sweden	4	0	2	6
United States	2	1	3	6
Italy	2	1	2	5
Norway	0	3	2	5
Canada	0	2	3	5
Yugoslavia	0	2	1	3
Czechoslovakia	0	1	2	3
France	1	0	1	2
Japan	0	0	1	1
Liechtenstein	0	0	1	1

CANADA'S WINTER MEDALISTS

	Competitor	Medal	Event
1924 Chamonix	Toronto Granites	gold	hockey
1928 St. Moritz	Toronto Graduates	gold	hockey
1932 Lake Placid	The Winnipegs	gold	hockey
	Alex Hurd	silver	speed skating, 1500 m
	Alex Hurd	bronze	speed skating, 500 m
	William Logan	bronze	speed skating, 1500 m
	William Logan	bronze	speed skating, 5000 m
	Frank Stack	bronze	speed skating, 10 000 m
	Montgomery Wilson	bronze	figure skating, singles
1936 Garmisch-Partenkirchen	Port Arthur Bearcats	silver	hockey
1948 St. Moritz	RCAF Flyers	gold	hockey
	Barbara Ann Scott	gold	figure skating, singles
	Suzanne Morrow/ Wallace Diestelmeyer	bronze	figure skating, pairs
1952 Oslo	Edmonton Mercurys	gold	hockey
	Gord Audley	bronze	speed skating, 500 m
1956 Cortina d'Ampezzo	Frances Dafoe/ Norris Bowden	silver	figure skating, pairs
	Lucille Wheeler	bronze	alpine skiing, downhill
	Kitchener-Waterloo Dutchmen	bronze	hockey
1960 Squaw Valley	Anne Heggtveit	gold	alpine skiing, slalom
	Barbara Wagner/ Robert Paul	gold	figure skating, pairs
	Kitchener-Waterloo Dutchmen	silver	hockey
	Donald Jackson	bronze	figure skating, singles
1964 Innsbruck	Vic Emery/ John Emery/ Doug Anakin/ Peter Kirby	gold	bobsleigh, four-man
	Petra Burka	bronze	figure skating, singles
	Debbi Wilkes/ Guy Revell	bronze	figure skating, pairs
1968 Grenoble	Nancy Greene	gold	alpine skiing, giant slalom
	Nancy Greene	silver	alpine skiing, slalom
	Canadian National Team	bronze	hockey
1972 Sapporo	Karen Magnussen	silver	figure skating, singles
1976 Innsbruck	Kathy Kreiner	gold	alpine skiing, giant slalom
	Cathy Priestner	silver	speed skating, 500 m
	Toller Cranston	bronze	figure skating, singles
1980 Lake Placid	Gaetan Boucher	silver	speed skating, 1000 m
	Steve Podborski	bronze	alpine skiing, downhill
1984 Sarajevo	Gaetan Boucher	gold	speed skating, 1000 m
	Gaetan Boucher	gold	speed skating, 1500 m
	Gaetan Boucher	bronze	speed skating, 500 m
	Brian Orser	silver	figure skating, singles
1988 Calgary	Brian Orser	silver	figure skating, singles
	Elizabeth Manley	silver	figure skating, singles
	Karen Percy	bronze	alpine skiing, downhill
	Karen Percy	bronze	alpine skiing, Super G
	Tracy Wilson/ Rob McCall	bronze	figure skating, ice dancing

The athletes of Canada at the Opening Ceremony.

ABBREVIATIONS

Countries

AHO	Netherlands Antilles	JAM	Jamaica
AND	Andorra	JPN	Japan
ARG	Argentina	KOR	Korea
AUS	Australia	LIB	Lebanon
AUT	Austria	LIE	Liechtenstein
BEL	Belgium	LUX	Luxembourg
BOL	Bolivia	MEX	Mexico
BUL	Bulgaria	MON	Monaco
CAN	Canada	MGL	Mongolia
CHI	Chile	MAR	Morocco
TPE	Chinese Taipei	HOL	Netherlands
CRC	Costa Rica	NZL	New Zealand
CYP	Cyprus	NOR	Norway
TCH	Czechoslovakia	CHN	People's Republic
PRK	Democratic People's		of China
	Republic of Korea	PHI	Philippines
DEN	Denmark	POL	Poland
FRG	Federal Republic of	POR	Portugal
	Germany	PUR	Puerto Rico
FIJ	Fiji	ROM	Romania
FIN	Finland	SMR	San Marino
FRA	France	ESP	Spain
GDR	German Democratic	SWE	Sweden
	Republic	SUI	Switzerland
GBR	Great Britain	TUR	Turkey
GRE	Greece	USA	United States
GUA	Guatemala	URS	USSR
GUM	Guam	ISV	Virgin Islands
HUN	Hungary	YUG	Yugoslavia
ISL	Iceland	Results	
IND	India	DIS	Disqualified
ITA	Italy	DNF	Did Not Finish

ALPINE SKIING

Alpine skiing was introduced to North America by Scandinavian immigrants in the late nineteenth century, but surprisingly it was not until 1948 that downhill and slalom were included in the Olympic Winter Games as separate events. During the 1988 Games, events for both men and women included the downhill, slalom, giant slalom, super giant slalom, and alpine combination.

Competitions took place on Nakiska at Mount Allan, a new skiing area developed during the 1986-87 winter season and offering some of the finest courses ever designed for Olympic competition.

CANADIAN ALPINE TEAM

Currie Chapman	—women's head coach
Don Lyon	—women's downhill coach
Carl Petersen	—trainer
Kevin Albrecht	—team leader
Kellie Casey	—downhill
Nancy Gee	—combined
Laurie Graham	—downhill, Super G
Josee Lacasse	—slalom, giant slalom
Lucie Laroche	—downhill, Super G
Kerrin Lee	—downhill, slalom, giant slalom, Super G, combined
Michelle McKendry	—slalom, giant slalom, Super G, combined
Karen Percy	—downhill, slalom, giant slalom, Super G, combined
Glenn Wurtele	—men's head coach
Heinz Stohl	—men's downhill coach

Felix Belczyk	—downhill, Super G, combined
Peter Bosinger	—giant slalom
Robert Boyd	—downhill, Super G, combined
Mike Carney	—downhill
Greg Grossmann	—slalom, giant slalom
Daniel Moar	—downhill
Jim Read	—slalom, giant slalom, Super G
Brian Stemmle	—downhill, giant slalom, combined
Donald Stevens	—downhill, combined
Mike Tommy	—slalom, combined
Alain Villiard	—slalom, giant slalom, Super G

Men's Downhill (February 15)

1.	Pirmin Zurbriggen, SUI	1:59.63
2.	Peter Mueller, SUI	2.00.14
3.	Franck Piccard, FRA	2:01.24
4.	Leonard Stock, AUT	2:01.56
5.	Gerhard Pfaffenbichler, AUT	2:02.02
6.	Markus Wasmeier, FRG	2:02.03
7.	Anton Steiner, AUT	2:02.19
8.	Martin Bell, GBR	2:02.49
9.	Marc Girardelli, LUX	2:02.59
10.	Danilo Sbardellotto, ITA	2:02.69
14.	Michael Carney, CAN	2:03.25
16.	Rob Boyd, CAN	2:03.27
18.	Felix Belczyk, CAN	2:03.59
DIS	Brian Stemmle, CAN	

Men's Combined (February 16 & 17)

		Downhill	Slalom	Total
1.	Hubert Strolz, AUT	17.77	18.78	36.55
2.	Bernhard Gstrein, AUT	36.43	7.02	43.45
3.	Paul Accola, SUI	48.24	0.00	48.24
4.	Luc Alphand, FRA	29.80	27.93	57.73
5.	Peter Jurko, TCH	37.42	21.14	58.56
6.	Jean-Luc Cretier, FRA	34.66	28.32	62.98
7.	Markus Wasmeier, FRG	26.71	38.73	65.44
8.	Adrian Bires, TCH	36.87	31.63	68.50
9.	Finn Jagge, NOR	85.66	9.55	95.21
10.	Niklas Henning, SWE	47.02	49.23	96.25
19.	Donald Stevens, CAN	44.93	90.88	135.81

Women's Downhill (February 19)

1.	Marina Kiehl, FRG	1:25.86
2.	Brigitte Oertli, SUI	1:26.61
3.	Karen Percy, CAN	1:26.62
4.	Maria Walliser, SUI	1:26.89
5.	Laurie Graham, CAN	1:26.99
6.	Petra Kronberger, AUT	1:27.03
7.	Regina Moesenlechner, FRG	1:27.16
8.	Elisabeth Kirchler, AUT	1:27.19
9.	Michela Figini, SUI	1:27.26
10.	Lucia Medzihradska, TCH	1:27.28
15.	Kerrin Lee, CAN	1:28.07
DNF	Kellie Casey, CAN	

Women's Combined (February 20 & 21)

		Downhill	Slalom	Total
1.	Anita Wachter, AUT	10.49	18.76	29.25
2.	Brigitte Oertli, SUI	29.48	0.00	29.48
3.	Maria Walliser, SUI	8.03	43.25	51.28
4.	Karen Percy, CAN	27.16	27.31	54.47
5.	Lenka Kebrlova, TCH	30.40	30.47	60.87
6.	Lucia Medzihradska, TCH	33.34	30.22	63.56
7.	Michelle McKendry, CAN	17.28	47.57	64.85
8.	Kerrin Lee, CAN	26.08	39.18	65.26
9.	Ulrike Stanggassinger, FRG	22.53	48.98	71.51
10.	Michaela Marzola, ITA	23.00	62.34	85.34
13.	Nancy Gee, CAN	57.87	45.99	103.86

Men's Super Giant Slalom (February 21)

1.	Franck Piccard, FRA	1:39.66
2.	Helmut Mayer, AUT	1:40.96
3.	Lars Borje Eriksson, SWE	1:41.08
4.	Hubert Strolz, AUT	1:41.11
5.	Pirmin Zurbriggen, SUI	1:41.96
5.	Guenther Mader, AUT	1:41.96
7.	Luc Alphand, FRA	1:42.27
8.	Leonard Stock, AUT	1:42.36
9.	Tomaz Cizman, YUG	1:42.47
10.	Ivano Camozzi, ITA	1:42.66
13.	Jim Read, CAN	1:43.01
19.	Felix Belczyk, CAN	1:44.31
22.	Rob Boyd, CAN	1:45.04
DNF	Alain Villiard, CAN	

Women's Super Giant Slalom (February 22)

1.	Sigrid Wolf, AUT	1:19.03
2.	Michela Figini, SUI	1:20.03
3.	Karen Percy, CAN	1:20.29
4.	Regina Moesenlechner, FRG	1:20.33
5.	Anita Wachter, AUT	1:20.36
6.	Maria Walliser, SUI	1:20.48
7.	Michaela Marzola, ITA	1:20.91
7.	Zoe Haas, SUI	1:20.91
9.	Edith Thys, USA	1:20.93
10.	Christa Kinshofer-Guethlein, FRG	1:20.98
10.	Elisabeth Gerg, FRG	1:20.98
13.	Laurie Graham, CAN	1:21.11
19.	Lucie Laroche, CAN	1:21.95
23.	Kerrin Lee, CAN	1:22.11

Women's Giant Slalom (February 24)

1.	Vreni Schneider, SUI	2:06.49
2.	Christa Kinshofer-Guethlein, FRG	2:07.42
3.	Maria Walliser, SUI	2:07.72
4.	Mateja Svet, YUG	2:07.80
5.	Christine Meier, FRG	2:07.88
6.	Ulrike Maier, AUT	2:08.10
7.	Anita Wachter, AUT	2:08.38
8.	Catherine Quittet, FRA	2:08.84
9.	Carole Merle, FRA	2:09.36
10.	Christelle Guignard, FRA	2:09.46
11.	Josee Lacasse, CAN	2:09.78
17.	Kerrin Lee, CAN	2:13.32
DNF	Karen Percy, CAN	
DNF	Michelle McKendry, CAN	

Men's Giant Slalom (February 25)

1.	Alberto Tomba, ITA	2:06.37
2.	Hubert Strolz, AUT	2:07.41
3.	Pirmin Zurbriggen, SUI	2:08.39
4.	Ivano Camozzi, ITA	2:08.77
5.	Rudolf Nierlich, AUT	2:08.92
6.	Andreas Wenzel, LIE	2:09.03
7.	Helmut Mayer, AUT	2:09.09
8.	Frank Woerndl, FRG	2:09.22
9.	Rok Petrovic, YUG	2:09.32
10.	Joel Gaspoz, SUI	2:09.57
DIS	Jim Read, CAN	
DIS	Alain Villiard, CAN	
DIS	Peter Bosinger, CAN	
DIS	Greg Grossmann, CAN	

Women's Slalom (February 26)

1.	Vreni Schneider, SUI	1:36.69
2.	Mateja Svet, YUG	1:38.37
3.	Christa Kinshofer-Guethlein, FRG	1:38.40
4.	Roswitha Steiner, AUT	1:38.77
5.	Blanca Fernandez Ochoa, ESP	1:39.44
6.	Ida Ladstaetter, AUT	1:39.59
7.	Paoletta Magoni Sforza, ITA	1:39.76
8.	Dorota Mogore Tlalka, FRA	1:39.86
9.	Mojca Dezman, YUG	1:40.21
10.	Ulrike Maier, AUT	1:40.54
16.	Josee Lacasse, CAN	1:43.14
18.	Michelle McKendry, CAN	1:45.79
DNF	Karen Percy, CAN	
DIS	Kerrin Lee, CAN	

Men's Slalom (February 27)

1.	Alberto Tomba, ITA	1:39.47
2.	Frank Woerndl, FRG	1:39.53
3.	Paul Frommelt, LIE	1:39.84
4.	Bernhard Gstrein, AUT	1:40.08
5.	Ingemar Stenmark, SWE	1:40.22
6.	Jonas Nilsson, SWE	1:40.23
7.	Pirmin Zurbriggen, SUI	1:40.48
8.	Oswald Totsch, ITA	1:40.55
9.	Grega Benedik, YUG	1:41.38
10.	Florian Beck, FRG	1:41.44
14.	Alain Villiard, CAN	1:43.77
DNF	Mike Tommy, CAN	
DNF	Greg Grossmann, CAN	
DNF	Jim Read, CAN	

BIATHLON

Biathlon was one of the earliest Olympic events but was dropped in 1948 because of its military associations. Since it was reintroduced to Olympic competition in 1960, the event has been dominated by Sweden, Norway, Finland, the German Democratic Republic, the Soviet Union, and the Federal Republic of Germany. In 1988, three competitions were held at the Canmore Nordic Centre: the 10-kilometre and the 20-kilometre races, and the four-man relay.

In recent years the classic skiing technique of the diagonal stride has been replaced to a large extent by the free skating technique, resulting in faster speeds in the event. The use of a .22-calibre rifle was standardized in 1978.

CANADIAN BIATHLON TEAM

Hans Skinstad	—head coach
Pierre Pepin	—assistant coach
Dr. John Edwards	—team leader

Jamie Kallio
Ken Karpoff
Charles Plamondon
Glenn Rupertus
Paget Stewart

20-kilometre (February 20)

1.	Frank-Peter Roetsch, GDR	56:33.3
2.	Valeri Medvedtsev, URS	56:54.6
3.	Johann Passler, ITA	57:10.1
4.	Serguei Tchepikov, URS	57:17.5
5.	Yuri Kashkarov, URS	57:43.1
6.	Eirik Kvalfoss, NOR	57:54.6
7.	Andre Sehmisch, GDR	58:11.4
8.	Tapio Piipponen, FIN	58:18.3
9.	Matthias Jacob, GDR	58:20.1
10.	Peter Angerer, FRG	58:46.7
33.	Ken Karpoff, CAN	1:02:19.7
34.	Glenn Rupertus, CAN	1:03:10.4
46.	Charles Plamondon, CAN	1:04:27.5
59.	Jamie Kallio, CAN	1:10:13.1

10-kilometre (February 23)

1.	Frank-Peter Roetsch, GDR	25:08.1
2.	Valeri Medvedtsev, URS	25:23.7
3.	Serguei Tchepikov, URS	25:29.4
4.	Birk Anders, GDR	25:51.8
5.	Andre Sehmisch, GDR	25:52.3
6.	Frank Luck, GDR	25:57.6
7.	Tapio Piipponen, FIN	26:02.2
8.	Johann Passler, ITA	26:07.7
9.	Dmitri Vassiliev, URS	26:09.7
10.	Peter Angerer, FRG	26:13.2
34.	Glenn Rupertus, CAN	27:38.6
46.	Ken Karpoff, CAN	28:12.9
55.	Charles Plamondon, CAN	28:30.5
58.	Paget Stewart, CAN	29:06.9

4-x-7.5-kilometre Relay (February 26)

		Team Time
1.	D. Vassiliev, S. Tchepikov, A. Popov, V. Medvedtsev, URS	1:22:30.0
2.	E. Reiter, S. Hoeck, P. Angerer, F. Fischer, FRG	1:23:37.4
3.	W. Kiem, G. Taschler, J. Passler, A. Zingerle, ITA	1:23:51.5
4.	A. Lengauer Stockner, B. Hofstaetter, F. Schuler, A. Eder, AUT	1:24:17.6
5.	J. Wirth, F. Roetsch, M. Jacob, A. Sehmisch, GDR	1:24:28.4
6.	G. Einang, F. Loberg, G. Fenne, E. Kvalfoss, NOR	1:25:57.0
7.	P. Sjoden, M. Lofgren, R. Westling, L. Andersson, SWE	1:29:11.9
8.	V. Bojilov, V. Velitchkov, K. Videnov, H. Vodenitcharov, BUL	1:29:24.9
9.	L. Nelson, C. Schreiner, D. Binning, J. Thompson, USA	1:29:33.0
10.	E. Claudon, J. Giachino, H. Flandin, F. Mougel, FRA	1:30:22.8
15.	C. Plamondon, G. Rupertus, K. Karpoff, J. Kallio, CAN	1:33:37.0

BOBSLEIGH

The four-man bobsleigh event was introduced at the first Olympic Winter Games in Chamonix, France, in 1924; eight years later, at Lake Placid, New York, the two-man bob event was added. The high point in Canadian Olympic bobsleigh competition was the surprise gold medal won in 1964 by the team of Victor Emery, John Emery, Peter Kirby, and Douglas Anakin.

The newly designed track at Canada Olympic Park, which combines bobsleigh and luge, has fourteen corners. On three curves, a force of more than four g's is exerted on bobsledders. The track also features the latest technology, including more than a hundred computer-controlled timing lights along the length of the track.

CANADIAN BOBSLEIGH TEAM

Werner Delle-Karth	–head coach
Georg Werth	–assistant coach
Greg Alford	–team leader
Howard Dell	–brakeman
John Graham	–brakeman
Lloyd Guss	–brakeman
Greg Haydenluck	–driver
Cal Langford	–crewman
Ken LeBlanc	–crewman
David Leuty	–driver
Chris Lori	–driver
Andrew Mowatt	–crewman
Peter Stovel	–crewman
Andy Swim	–crewman
Kevin Tyler	–crewman

Two-man (February 20 & 22)

1.	I. Kipours, V. Kozlov, URS-I	3:53.48
2.	W. Hoppe, B. Musiol, GDR-I	3:54.19
3.	B. Lehmann, M. Hoyer, GDR-II	3:54.64
4.	G. Weder, D. Acklin, SUI-II	3:56.06
5.	I. Appelt, H. Winkler, AUT-I	3:56.49
6.	H. Hiltebrand, A. Kiser, SUI-I	3:56.52
7.	A. Fischer, C. Langen, FRG-I	3:56.62
8.	P. Kienast, C. Mark, AUT-II	3:56.91
9.	Z. Ekmanis, A. Trops, URS-II	3:56.92
10.	G. Haydenluck, L. Guss, CAN-I	3:56.97
13.	D. Leuty, K. Tyler, CAN-II	3:58.19

Four-man (February 27 & 28)

1.	E. Fasser, K. Meier, M. Faessler, W. Stocker, SUI-I	3:47.51
2.	W. Hoppe, D. Schauerhammer, B. Musiol, I. Voge, GDR-I	3:47.58
3.	I. Kipours, G. Ossis, I. Tone, V. Kozlov, URS-II	3:48.26
4.	B. Rushlaw, H. Hoye, M. Wasko, W. White, USA-I	3:48.28
5.	M. Poikans, O. Kliavinch, I. Berzoups, I. Iaoudzems, URS-I	3:48.35
6.	P. Kienast, F. Siegl, C. Mark, K. Teigl, AUT-I	3:48.65
7.	I. Appelt, J. Muigg, G. Redl, H. Winkler, AUT-II	3:48.95
8.	D. Richter, B. Ferl, L. Jahn, A. Szelig, GDR-II	3:49.06
9.	H. Hiltebrand, U. Fehlmann, E. Fassbind, A. Kiser, SUI-II	3:49.25
10.	A. Wolf, P. Gesuito, G. Beikircher, S. Ticci, ITA-I	3:49.46
13.	G. Haydenluck, C. Langford, K. Tyler, L. Guss, CAN-II	3:49.99
15.	C. Lori, K. LeBlanc, A. Swim, H. Dell, CAN-I	3:50.37

CROSS-COUNTRY SKIING

The oldest Olympic skiing competition, cross-country racing has been a part of every Winter Games. Four countries–the Soviet Union, Finland, Norway, and Sweden–have traditionally dominated this event.

In 1988, thirty-four countries competed at Canmore Nordic Centre in competitions consisting of individual races of varying distances for both men and women, and two relay races.

CANADIAN CROSS-COUNTRY SKIING TEAM

Laurent Roux	–head coach
Jack Sasseville	–assistant coach
Tracy Bell	–physiotherapist
Marty Hall	–team leader

Carol Gibson
Marie Andree Masson
Jean McAllister
Lorna Sasseville
Angela Schmidt Foster

Yves Bilodeau
Wayne Dustin
Pierre Harvey
Dennis Lawrence
Alain Masson
Alan Pilcher

Women's 10-kilometre (February 14)

1.	Vida Ventsene, URS	30:08.3
2.	Raisa Smetanina, URS	30:17.0
3.	Marjo Matikainen, FIN	30:20.5
4.	Svetlana Nagueikina, URS	30:26.5
5.	Tamara Tikhonova, URS	30:38.9
6.	Inger Helene Nybraten, NOR	30:51.7
7.	Pirkko Maatta, FIN	30:52.4

8.	Marie Helene Westin, SWE	30:53.5
9.	Marja Liisa Kirvesniemi, FIN	30:57.0
10.	Simone Opitz, GDR	31:14.3
30.	Lorna Sasseville, CAN	32:49.7
33.	Carol Gibson, CAN	33:03.9
37.	Marie Andree Masson, CAN	33:35.6
38.	Angela Schmidt Foster, CAN	33:45.9

Men's 30-kilometre (February 15)

1.	Alexei Prokourorov, URS	1:24:26.3
2.	Vladimir Smirnov, URS	1:24:35.1
3.	Vegard Ulvang, NOR	1:25:11.6
4.	Mikhail Deviatiarov, URS	1:25:31.3
5.	Giorgio Vanzetta, ITA	1:25:37.2
6.	Pal Mikkelsplass, NOR	1:25:44.6
7.	Gianfranco Polvara, ITA	1:26:02.7
8.	Marco Albarello, ITA	1:26:09.1
9.	Harri Kirvesniemi, FIN	1:26:59.6
10.	Gunde Svan, SWE	1:27:30.8
14.	Pierre Harvey, CAN	1:28:21.7
35.	Yves Bilodeau, CAN	1:32:17.8
39.	Al Pilcher, CAN	1:33:04.7
46.	Wayne Dustin, CAN	1:34:37.8

Women's 5-kilometre (February 17)

1.	Marjo Matikainen, FIN	15:04.0
2.	Tamara Tikhonova, URS	15:05.3
3.	Vida Ventsene, URS	15:11.1
4.	Anne Jahren, NOR	15:12.6
5.	Marja Liisa Kirvesniemi, FIN	15:16.7
6.	Inger Helene Nybraten, NOR	15:17.7
7.	Marie Helene Westin, SWE	15:28.9
8.	Svetlana Nagueikina, URS	15:29.9
9.	Marianne Dahlmo, NOR	15:30.4
10.	Raisa Smetanina, URS	15:35.9
26.	Lorna Sasseville, CAN	16:23.3
32.	Angela Schmidt Foster, CAN	16:32.5
33.	Carol Gibson, CAN	16:35.2
46.	Jean McAllister, CAN	17:32.4

Men's 15-kilometre (February 19)

1.	Mikhail Deviatiarov, URS	41:18.9
2.	Pal Mikkelsplass, NOR	41:33.4
3.	Vladimir Smirnov, URS	41:48.5
4.	Oddvar Braa, NOR	42:17.3
5.	Uwe Bellmann, GDR	42:17.8
6.	Maurilio de Zolt, ITA	42:31.2
7.	Vegard Ulvang, NOR	42:31.5
8.	Harri Kirvesniemi, FIN	42:42.8
9.	Marco Albarello, ITA	42:48.6
10.	Giorgio Vanzetta, ITA	42:49.6
17.	Pierre Harvey, CAN	43:22.0
34.	Yves Bilodeau, CAN	45:26.6
46.	Al Pilcher, CAN	46:21.1
47.	Dennis Lawrence, CAN	46:26.3

Women's 4-x-5-kilometre Relay (February 21)

		Team Time
1.	S. Nagueikina, N. Gavriliuk, T. Tikhonova, A. Reztsova, URS	59:51.1
2.	T. Dybendahl, M. Wold, A. Jahren, M. Dahlmo, NOR	1:01:33.0
3.	P. Maatta, M. Kirvesniemi, M. Matikainen, J. Savolainen, FIN	1:01:53.8
4.	K. Thomas, S. Parpan, E. Kratzer, C. Gilli-Bruegger, SUI	1:01:59.4
5.	K. Moring, S. Opitz, S. Braun, S. Greiner Petter, GDR	1:02:19.9
6.	L. Frost, A. Fritzon, K. Lamberg-Skog, M. Westin, SWE	1:02:24.9
7.	L. Balazova, V. Klimkova, I. Radlova, A. Havrancikova, TCH	1:03:37.1

8.	D. Denhartog, L. Thompson, N. Fiddler, L. Krichko, USA	1:04:08.8
9.	A. Schmidt Foster, C. Gibson, L. Sasseville, M. Masson, CAN	1:04:22.6
10.	K. Angerer, G. Dal Sasso, E. Desderi, S. Belmondo, ITA	1:04:23.6

Men's 4-x-10-kilometre Relay (February 22)

		Team Time
1.	J. Ottosson, T. Wassberg, G. Svan, T. Mogren, SWE	1:43:58.6
2.	V. Smirnov, V. Sakhnov, M. Deviatiarov, A. Prokurorov, URS	1:44:11.3
3.	R. Nyc, V. Korunka, P. Benc, L. Svanda, TCH	1:45:22.7
4.	A. Gruenenfelder, J. Capol, G. Guidon, J. Wigger, SUI	1:46:16.3
5.	S. Barco, A. Walder, G. Vanzetta, M. de Zolt, ITA	1:46:16.7
6.	P. Mikkelsplass, O. Braa, V. Ulvang, T. Langli, NOR	1:46:48.7
7.	W. Kuss, G. Fischer, J. Behle, H. Fritzenwenger, FRG	1:48:05.0
8.	J. Laukkanen, H. Kirvesniemi, J. Rasanen, K. Ristanen, FIN	1:48:24.0
9.	Y. Bilodeau, A. Pilcher, P. Harvey, D. Lawrence, CAN	1:48:59.7
10.	A. Blatter, A. Schwarz, J. Standmann, A. Stadlober, AUT	1:49:14.5

Women's 20-kilometre (February 25)

1.	Tamara Tikhonova, URS	55:53.6
2.	Anfissa Reztsova, URS	56:12.8
3.	Raisa Smetanina, URS	57:22.1
4.	Christina Gilli-Bruegger, SUI	57:37.4
5.	Simone Opitz, GDR	57:54.3
6.	Manuela di Centa, ITA	57:55.2
7.	Kerstin Moring, GDR	58:17.2
8.	Marianne Dahlmo, NOR	58:31.1
9.	Anna-Lena Fritzon, SWE	58:37.4
10.	Marie Helene Westin, SWE	58:39.4
26.	Carol Gibson, CAN	1:01:12.0
27.	Marie Andree Masson, CAN	1:01:12.6
31.	Jean McAllister, CAN	1:02:02.8
44.	Angela Schmidt Foster, CAN	1:04:21.9

Men's 50-kilometre (February 27)

1.	Gunde Svan, SWE	2:04:30.9
2.	Maurilio de Zolt, ITA	2:05:36.4
3.	Andy Gruenenfelder, SUI	2:06:01.9
4.	Vegard Ulvang, NOR	2:06:32.3
5.	Holger Bauroth, GDR	2:07:02.4
6.	Jan Ottosson, SWE	2:07:34.8
7.	Kari Ristanen, FIN	2:08:08.1
8.	Uwe Bellmann, GDR	2:08:18.6
9.	Pal Mikkelsplass, NOR	2:08:20.0
10.	Gianfranco Polvara, ITA	2:08:40.3
21.	Pierre Harvey, CAN	2:10:54.8
43.	Dennis Lawrence, CAN	2:17:55.7
46.	Alain Masson, CAN	2:19:21.7
49.	Wayne Dustin, CAN	2:21:31.8

FIGURE SKATING

One of the most popular events at the Olympics, figure skating was a competitive sport before there were Olympic Winter Games. The 1988 Olympic Winter Games offered four events—women's singles, men's singles, pairs, and ice dancing, in addition to a non-competitive skating exhibition held on the last day of the Games.

Figure skating has one of the most complex scoring systems of any Olympic sport, and the judging of competition is often controversial and disputed by enthusiastic audiences. The Olympic Saddledome was the principal venue for figure skating competitions in Calgary.

CANADIAN FIGURE SKATING TEAM

Doug Leigh	–coach
Kerry Leitch	–pairs coach
Marijane Stong	–dance coach
Peter Jensen	–psychologist
Rosemary Marks	–assistant team leader
John M. McKay	–team leader
Elizabeth Manley	–singles (coaches: Peter Dunfield, Sonya Dunfield)
Charlene Wong	–singles (coaches: Peter Dunfield, Sonya Dunfield)
Kurt Browning	–singles (coach: Michael Jiranek)
Brian Orser	–singles (coach: Doug Leigh)
Neil Paterson	–singles (coach: Gary Paterson)
Lloyd Eisler & Isabelle Brasseur	–pairs (coach: Kerry Leitch) –pairs (coaches: Josee Picard, Eric Gillies)
Lyndon Johnston & Denise Benning	–pairs (coach: Kerry Leitch)
Doug Ladret & Christine Hough	–pairs (coach: Kerry Leitch)
Mike Farrington & Melanie Cole	–ice dance (coach: Roy Bradshaw)
Rod Garossino & Karyn Garossino	–ice dance (coaches: John Briscoe, Marijane Stong)
Rob McCall & Tracy Wilson	–ice dance (coaches: John Briscoe, Marijane Stong)

Pairs (February 14 & 16)

1. Ekaterina Gordeeva, Serguei Grinkov, URS
2. Elena Valova, Oleg Vassiliev, URS
3. Jill Watson, Peter Oppegard, USA
4. Larissa Selezneva, Oleg Makarov, URS
5. Gillian Wachsman, Todd Waggoner, USA
6. Denise Benning, Lyndon Johnston, CAN
7. Peggy Schwarz, Alexander Koenig, GDR
8. Christine Hough, Doug Ladret, CAN
9. Isabelle Brasseur, Lloyd Eisler, CAN
10. Natalie Seybold, Wayne Seybold, USA

Men's Singles (February 17, 18, & 20)

1. Brian Boitano, USA
2. Brian Orser, CAN
3. Victor Petrenko, URS
4. Alexandre Fadeev, URS
5. Grzegorz Filipowski, POL
6. Vladimir Kotin, URS
7. Christopher Bowman, USA
8. Kurt Browning, CAN
9. Heiko Fischer, FRG
10. Paul Wylie, USA
16. Neil Paterson, CAN

Ice Dancing (February 21, 22, & 23)

1. Natalia Bestemianova, Andrei Boukine, URS
2. Marina Klimova, Serguei Ponomarenko, URS
3. Tracy Wilson, Rob McCall, CAN
4. Natalia Annenko, Guenrikh Sretenski, URS
5. Kathrin Beck, Christoff Beck, AUT
6. Suzanne Semanick, Scott Gregory, USA
7. Klara Engi, Attila Toth, HUN
8. Isabelle Duchesnay, Paul Duchesnay, FRA
9. Antonia Becherer, Ferdinand Becherer, FRG
10. Lia Trovati, Roberto Pelizzola, ITA
12. Karyn Garossino, Rod Garossino, CAN
16. Melanie Cole, Mike Farrington, CAN

Women's Singles (February 24, 25, & 27)

1. Katarina Witt, GDR
2. Elizabeth Manley, CAN
3. Debi Thomas, USA
4. Jill Trenary, USA
5. Midori Ito, JPN
6. Claudia Leistner, FRG
7. Kira Ivanova, URS
8. Anna Kondracheva, URS
9. Simone Koch, GDR
10. Marina Kielmann, FRG
13. Charlene Wong, CAN

HOCKEY

From its first appearance as a demonstration sport in Antwerp, Belgium, during the 1920 VII Olympiad, hockey has grown into a fiercely contested Olympic event. Canada, the Soviet Union, and the United States have traditionally taken the gold medal in this event, the only exception being the 1936 gold medal awarded to Great Britain.

In 1988, twelve teams competed at Stampede Corral and the Olympic Saddledome, with additional nonmedal rounds being played at Father David Bauer Olympic Arena. The structurally unique Saddledome features the world's largest concrete suspended roof and allows excellent viewing from all parts of the arena.

CANADIAN ICE HOCKEY TEAM

Dave King	–head coach
Guy Charron	–assistant coach
Tom Watt	–assistant coach
Terry Kane	–physiotherapist
Bill Stefaniuk	–trainer
Ken Berry	–forward
Serge Boisvert	–forward
Brian Bradley	–forward
Sean Burke	–goaltender
Chris Felix	–defense
Randy Gregg	–defense
Marc Habscheid	–forward
Robert Joyce	–forward
Vaughn Karpan	–forward
Merlin Malinowski	–forward
Andy Moog	–goaltender
Jim Peplinski	–forward
Serge Roy	–defense
Wallace Schreiber	–forward
Gord Sherven	–forward
Tony Stiles	–defense
Steve Tambellini	–forward
Claude Vilgrain	–forward
Tim Watters	–defense
Ken Yaremchuk	–forward
Trent Yawney	–defense
Zarley Zalapski	–defense

Pool A Final Standings (February 13–25)

	Team	Win	Tie	Loss	GF	GA	Points
1.	Finland	3	1	1	22	8	7
2.	Sweden	2	3	0	23	10	7
3.	Canada	3	1	1	17	12	7
4.	Switzerland	3	0	2	19	10	6
5.	Poland	0	1	4	3	13	1
6.	France	1	0	4	10	41	0

Pool B Final Standings (February 13–25)

	Team	Win	Tie	Loss	GF	GA	Points
1.	Soviet Union	5	0	0	32	10	10
2.	Federal Republic of Germany	4	0	1	19	12	8
3.	Czechoslovakia	3	0	2	23	14	6
4.	United States	2	0	3	27	27	4
5.	Austria	0	1	4	12	29	1
5.	Norway	0	1	4	11	32	1

Final Medal Standings (February 24–28)

	Team	Win	Tie	Loss	GF	GA	Points
1.	Soviet Union	4	0	1	25	7	8
2.	Finland	3	1	1	18	10	7
3.	Sweden	2	2	1	15	16	6
4.	Canada	2	1	2	17	14	5
5.	Federal Republic of Germany	1	0	4	8	26	2
5.	Czechoslovakia	1	0	4	12	22	2

LUGE

First introduced as an Olympic event in 1964, luge is a relatively young sport in Canada. The new artificial track at Canada Olympic Park is the first in the country and is expected to encourage more Canadian interest and involvement in luge. In Calgary, Canada had a top-ten finish in two events, but the track was dominated by the German Democratic Republic.

One of the world's few combined luge/bobsleigh tracks, the Calgary track is equipped with more than 100 kilometres of refrigeration pipe which theoretically can keep the ice in race condition up to temperatures of 20 degrees Celsius. During the Calgary Olympics, however, record-high temperatures and sand-blowing winds necessitated reconditioning of the ice and forced one luge event and two bobsleigh events to be rescheduled.

CANADIAN LUGE TEAM

Carole Keyes	–coach
Franz Schachner	–assistant coach
Benoit Morin	–team leader

Marie Claude Doyon	–singles
Kathy Salmon	–singles

Andre Benoit	–doubles
Daniel Doll	–doubles
Robert Gasper	–doubles
Nil Labrecque	–singles
Harry Salmon	–doubles
Harington Telford	–singles
Chris Wightman	–singles

Men's Singles (February 14 & 15)

1.	Jens Mueller, GDR	3:05.548
2.	Georg Hackl, FRG	3:05.916
3.	Iouri Khartchenko, URS	3:06.274
4.	Thomas Jacob, GDR	3:06.358
5.	Michael Walter, GDR	3:06.933
6.	Serguei Daniline, URS	3:07.098
7.	Johannes Schettel, FRG	3:07.371
8.	Hansjorg Raffl, ITA	3:07.525
9.	Otto Mayregger, AUT	3:07.619
10.	Paul Hildgartner, ITA	3:07.696
19.	Harington Telford, CAN	3:09.298
24.	Chris Wightman, CAN	3:11.666
27.	Nil Labrecque, CAN	3:12.727

Women's Singles (February 16 & 18)

1.	Steffi Walter, GDR	3:03.973
2.	Ute Oberhoffner, GDR	3:04.105
3.	Cerstin Schmidt, GDR	3:04.181
4.	Veronika Bilgeri, FRG	3:05.670
5.	Ioulia Antipova, URS	3:05.787
6.	Bonny Warner, USA	3:06.056
7.	Marie Claude Doyon, CAN	3:06.211
8.	Nadejda Danilina, URS	3:06.364
9.	Cameron Myler, USA	3:06.835
10.	Irina Koussakina, URS	3.07.043
19.	Kathy Salmon, CAN	3:11.707

Doubles (February 19)

1.	J. Hoffmann, J. Pietzsch, GDR	1:31.940
2.	S. Krausse, J. Behrendt, GDR	1:32.039
3.	T. Schwab, W. Staudinger, FRG	1:32.274
4.	S. Ilsanker, G. Hackl, FRG	1:32.298
5.	G. Fluckinger, R. Manzenreiter, AUT	1:32.364
6.	V. Melnik, D. Alexeev, URS	1:32.459
7.	K. Brugger, W. Huber, ITA	1:32.553
7.	E. Belooussov, A. Beliakov, URS	1:32.553
9.	B. Kammerer, W. Brunner, ITA	1:33.171
10.	R. Gasper, A. Benoit, CAN	1:33.306
17.	H. Salmon, D. Doll, CAN	1:37.358

NORDIC COMBINED

Norway has usually dominated this event, which combines ski jumping and cross-country skiing. During the XV Olympic Winter Games, competitions were held at Canada Olympic Park and at the Canmore Nordic Centre, near Banff.

Each competing nation was allowed to enter four athletes in the individual nordic combined events and one team in the nordic combined combination relay, a new event introduced in 1988. Nordic combined has a different scoring system from other nordic events: cross-country skiing is judged on time, and jumping is judged on style and distance. Successful competitors must be equally skilled in both activities.

CANADIAN NORDIC COMBINED TEAM

Bjorn Bruvoll	–coach
Jean Dupre	–team leader

Jon Servold

Team Competition (February 23 & 24)

		Jump Team Points	3-x-10-kilometre Team Time
1.	H. Pohl, H. Schwarz, T. Mueller, FRG	629.8 (1)	1:20:46.0 (8)
2.	A. Schaad, H. Kempf, F. Glanzmann, SUI	571.4 (6)	1:15:57.4 (1)
3.	G. Csar, H. Aschenwald, K. Sulzenbacher, AUT	626.6 (2)	1:21:00.9 (9)
4.	H. Bogseth, T. Bredesen, T. Lokken, NOR	596.6 (3)	1:18:48.4 (3)
5.	T. Prenzel, M. Frank, U. Prenzel, GDR	571.6 (5)	1:18:13.5 (2)
6.	L. Patras, J. Klimko, M. Kopal, TCH	573.5 (4)	1:19:02.1 (4)
7.	P. Saapunki, J. Parviainen, J. Ylipulli, FIN	561.3 (7)	1:19:56.3 (7)
8.	J. Bohard, X. Girard, F. Guy, FRA	541.0 (8)	1:19:45.4 (5)
9.	H. Miyazaki, M. Abe, K. Kodama, JPN	515.3 (10)	1:19:54.3 (6)

10.	J. Holland, T. Wilson, H. Johnstone, USA	516.9 (9)	1:23:42.9 (10)

Individual Competition (February 28)

		Jump Points	15-kilometre Time
1.	Hippolyt Kempf, SUI	217.9 (3)	38:16.8 (2)
2.	Klaus Sulzenbacher, AUT	228.5 (1)	39:46.5 (17)
3.	Allar Levandi, URS	216.6 (4)	39:12.4 (12)
4.	Uwe Prenzel, GDR	207.6 (13)	38:18.8 (4)
5.	Andreas Schaad, SUI	207.2 (14)	38:18.0 (3)
6.	Torbjorn Lokken, NOR	199.4 (19)	37:39.0 (1)
7.	Miroslav Kopal, TCH	208.7 (12)	38:48.0 (8)
8.	Marko Frank, GDR	209.4 (10)	39:08.2 (11)
9.	Thomas Prenzel, GDR	215.5 (5)	39:51.4 (20)
10.	Vassili Savine, URS	203.7 (17)	38:37.5 (6)
38.	Jon Servold, CAN	187.1 (33)	41:56.1 (38)

SKI JUMPING

This sport has long been associated with Scandinavian countries and has been a popular Olympic event since 1924. The XV Olympic Winter Games in Calgary awarded medals in three events: the individual 70-metre and 90-metre jumps and the 90-metre team competition, the latter held for the first time.

Ski jumping took place at Canada Olympic Park to the enjoyment of huge crowds. The site became controversial during the Games because frequent high winds resulted in postponement of several competitions.

CANADIAN SKI JUMPING TEAM

Randy Richards	—coach
Jean Dupre	—team leader

Horst Bulau
Steve Collins
Todd Gillman
Ron Rautio
Ron Richards

70-metre (February 14)

1.	Matti Nykanen, FIN	229.1
2.	Pavel Ploc, TCH	212.1
3.	Jiri Malec, TCH	211.8
4.	Miran Tepes, YUG	211.2
5.	Jiri Parma, TCH	203.8
6.	Heinz Kuttin, AUT	199.7
7.	Jari Puikkonen, FIN	199.1
8.	Staffan Tallberg, SWE	198.1
9.	Jens Weissflog, GDR	196.6
10.	Piotr Fijas, POL	195.4
13.	Steve Collins, CAN	191.1
32.	Ron Richards, CAN	175.3
42.	Todd Gillman, CAN	171.0
44.	Horst Bulau, CAN	167.7

90-metre (February 23)

1.	Matti Nykanen, FIN	224.0
2.	Erik Johnsen, NOR	207.9
3.	Matjaz Debelak, YUG	207.7
4.	Thomas Klauser, FRG	205.1
5.	Pavel Ploc, TCH	204.1
6.	Andreas Felder, AUT	203.9
7.	Horst Bulau, CAN	197.6

8.	Staffan Tallberg, SWE	196.6
9.	Matjaz Zupan, YUG	195.8
10.	Miran Tepes, YUG	194.8
35.	Steve Collins, CAN	169.1
53.	Ron Richards, CAN	128.1
54.	Todd Gillman, CAN	110.8

90-metre Team (February 24)

		Team Points
1.	A. Nikkola, M. Nykanen, T. Ylipulli, J. Puikkonen, FIN	634.4
2.	P. Ulaga, M. Zupan, M. Debelak, M. Tepes, YUG	625.5
3.	O. Eidhammer, J. Kjorum, O. Fidjestol, E. Johnsen, NOR	596.1
4.	L. Dluhos, J. Malec, P. Ploc, J. Parma, TCH	586.8
5.	E. Vettori, H. Kuttin, G. Stranner, A. Felder, AUT	577.6
6.	A. Bauer, P. Rohwein, T. Klauser, J. Heumann, FRG	559.0
7.	P. Tallberg, A. Daun, J. Boklov, S. Tallberg, SWE	539.7
8.	G. Balanche, C. Lehmann, F. Piazzini, C. Hauswirth, SUI	516.1
9.	H. Bulau, S. Collins, T. Gillman, R. Richards, CAN	497.2
10.	T. Langlois, M. Konopacke, D. McGrane, M. Holland, USA	496.8

SPEED SKATING

This competition was one of the original events in the first Olympic Winter Games in Chamonix, France, in 1924. The Europeans and Soviets dominated the sport in the early years and continue to be successful in Olympic competition despite strong challenges from Canadian and American speed skaters.

The 1988 competitions, comprising five separate distances for men and women, were held in the magnificent new Olympic Oval, the world's largest and finest fully enclosed 400-metre speed skating oval. Its controlled environment led to a number of new world records in the event.

CANADIAN SPEED SKATING TEAM

Andrew Barron	—women's coach
Marcel Charland	—therapist
Don Wilson	—team leader

Chantal Cote	—1500 m, 3000 m
Kathy Gordon	—5000 m
Natalie Grenier	—500 m, 1000 m, 1500 m, 3000 m, 5000 m
Marie Pierre Lamarche	—1000 m
Ariane Loignon	—500 m, 1000 m, 1500 m, 3000 m, 5000 m
Caroline Maheux	—1500 m
Shelley Rhead	—500 m, 1000 m

Jack Walters	—men's coach

Gaetan Boucher	—500 m, 1000 m, 1500 m
Gordon Goplen	—5000 m, 10 000 m
Gregor Jelonek	—1500 m
Benoit Lamarche	—1500 m, 5000 m, 10 000 m
Jean Pichette	—1000 m, 1500 m, 5000 m, 10 000 m
Guy Thibault	—500 m, 1000 m
Marcel Tremblay	—1000 m
Robert Tremblay	—500 m
Daniel Turcotte	—500 m

Men's 500-metres (February 14)

1.	Jens-Uwe Mey, GDR	36.45
2.	Jan Ykema, HOL	36.76
3.	Akira Kuroiwa, JPN	36.77
4.	Serguei Fokitchev, URS	36.82

5.	Ki Tae Bae, KOR	36.90
6.	Igor Gelezovsky, URS	36.94
7.	Guy Thibault, CAN	36.96
8.	Nick Thometz, USA	37.16
9.	Yasumitsu Kanehama, JPN	37.25
10.	Frode Ronning, NOR	37.31
14.	Gaetan Boucher, CAN	37.47
17.	Daniel Turcotte, CAN	37.60
29.	Robert Tremblay, CAN	38.34

Men's 5000-metres (February 17)

1.	Tomas Gustafson, SWE	6:44.63
2.	Leendert Visser, HOL	6:44.98
3.	Gerard Kemkers, HOL	6:45.92
4.	Eric Flaim, USA	6:47.09
5.	Michael Hadschieff, AUT	6:48.72
6.	David Silk, USA	6:49.95
7.	Geir Karlstad, NOR	6:50.88
8.	Roland Freier, GDR	6:51.42
9.	Mark Greenwald, USA	6:51.98
10.	Danny Kah, AUS	6:52.14
21.	Benoit Lamarche, CAN	6:57.63
31.	Jean Pichette, CAN	7:04.95
34.	Gordon Goplen, CAN	7:08.49

Men's 1000-metres (February 18)

1.	Nikolai Gouliaev, URS	1:13.03
2.	Jens-Uwe Mey, GDR	1:13.11
3.	Igor Gelezovsky, URS	1:13.19
4.	Eric Flaim, USA	1:13.53
5.	Gaetan Boucher, CAN	1:13.77
6.	Michael Hadschieff, AUT	1:13.84
7.	Guy Thibault, CAN	1:14.16
8.	Peter Adeberg, GDR	1:14.19
9.	Yasumitsu Kanehama, JPN	1:14.36
9.	Ki Tae Bae, KOR	1:14.36
19.	Jean Pichette, CAN	1:14.72
22.	Marcel Tremblay, CAN	1.15.13

Men's 1500-metres (February 20)

1.	Andre Hoffmann, GDR	1:52.06
2.	Eric Flaim, USA	1:52.12
3.	Michael Hadschieff, AUT	1:52.31
4.	Igor Gelezovsky, URS	1:52.63
5.	Toru Aoyanagi, JPN	1:52.85
6.	Alexandre Klimov, URS	1:52.97
7.	Nikolai Gouliaev, URS	1:53.04
8.	Peter Adeberg, GDR	1:53.57
9.	Gaetan Boucher, CAN	1:54.18
10.	Jean Pichette, CAN	1:54.63
18.	Benoit Lamarche, CAN	1:55.59
23.	Gregor Jelonek, CAN	1:56.37

Men's 10 000-metres (February 21)

1.	Tomas Gustafson, SWE	13:48.20
2.	Michael Hadschieff, AUT	13:56.11
3.	Leendert Visser, HOL	14:00.55
4.	Eric Flaim, USA	14:05.57
5.	Gerard Kemkers, HOL	14:08.34
6.	Iouri Kliouev, URS	14:09.68
7.	Roberto Sighel, ITA	14:13.60
8.	Roland Freier, GDR	14:19.16
9.	Serguei Berezine, URS	14:20.48
10.	Benoit Lamarche, CAN	14:21.39
20.	Gordon Goplen, CAN	14:31.18

Women's 500-metres (February 22)

1.	Bonnie Blair, USA	39.10
2.	Christa Rothenburger, GDR	39.12
3.	Karin Kania, GDR	39.24
4.	Angela Stahnke, GDR	39.68
5.	Seiko Hashimoto, JPN	39.74
6.	Shelley Rhead, CAN	40.36
7.	Monika Holzner-Gawenus, FRG	40.53
8.	Shoko Fusano, JPN	40.61
9.	Natalia Chive, URS	40.66
10.	Andrea Ehrig, GDR	40.71
11.	Natalie Grenier, CAN	40.73
23.	Ariane Loignon, CAN	41.57

Women's 3000-metres (February 23)

1.	Yvonne van Gennip, HOL	4:11.94
2.	Andrea Ehrig, GDR	4:12.09
3.	Gabi Zange, GDR	4:16.92
4.	Karin Kania, GDR	4:18.80
5.	Erwina Rys Ferens, POL	4:22.59
6.	Svetlana Boiko, URS	4:22.90
7.	Seiko Hashimoto, JPN	4:23.29
7.	Elena Lapouga, URS	4:23.29
9.	Elena Toumanova, URS	4:24.07
10.	Jasmin Krohn, SWE	4:25.06
15.	Ariane Loignon, CAN	4:28.55
26.	Chantal Cote, CAN	4:35.74

Women's 1000-metres (February 26)

1.	Christa Rothenburger, GDR	1:17.65
2.	Karin Kania, GDR	1:17.70
3.	Bonnie Blair, USA	1:18.31
4.	Andrea Ehrig, GDR	1:19.32
5.	Seiko Hashimoto, JPN	1:19.75
6.	Angela Stahnke, GDR	1:20.05
7.	Leslie Bader, USA	1:21.09
8.	Katie Class, USA	1:21.10
9.	Natalie Grenier, CAN	1:21.15
10.	Erwina Rys Ferens, POL	1:21.44
14.	Shelley Rhead, CAN	1:21.84
19.	Ariane Loignon, CAN	1:22.75
25.	Marie Pierre Lamarche, CAN	1:25.18

Women's 1500-metres (February 27)

1.	Yvonne van Gennip, HOL	2:00.68
2.	Karin Kania, GDR	2:00.82
3.	Andrea Ehrig, GDR	2:01.49
4.	Bonnie Blair, USA	2:04.02
5.	Elena Lapouga, URS	2:04.24
6.	Seiko Hashimoto, JPN	2:04.38
7.	Gunda Kleemann, GDR	2:04.68
7.	Erwina Rys Ferens, POL	2:04.68
9.	Hwa Song, PRK	2:05.25
10.	Leslie Bader, USA	2:05.53
11.	Natalie Grenier, CAN	2:06.80
14.	Ariane Loignon, CAN	2:07.63
21.	Chantal Cote, CAN	2:09.62
23.	Caroline Maheux, CAN	2:10.83

Women's 5000-metres (February 28)

1.	Yvonne van Gennip, HOL	7:14.13
2.	Andrea Ehrig, GDR	7:17.12
3.	Gabi Zange, GDR	7:21.61
4.	Svetlana Boiko, URS	7:28.39
5.	Elena Lapouga, URS	7:28.65
6.	Seiko Hashimoto, JPN	7:34.43
7.	Gunda Kleemann, GDR	7:34.59
8.	Jasmin Krohn, SWE	7:36.56
9.	Chun Han, PRK	7:36.81
10.	Janet Goldman, USA	7:36.98
18.	Natalie Grenier, CAN	7:46.96
20.	Ariane Loignon, CAN	7:49.55
23.	Kathy Gordon, CAN	7:53.30

PHOTO CREDITS

One of the Federal Republic of Germany's four-man bobsleigh teams.